1–3 JOHN: A GENERAL READER

1–3 John
A GENERAL READER

1 John	J. Klay Harrison
2–3 John	Chad M. Foster

GLOSSAHOUSE
WILMORE, KY $\quad$ G_H
WWW.GLOSSAHOUSE.COM

1–3 John: A General Reader

GlossaHouse, LLC
110 Callis Circle
Wilmore, KY 40390

Harrison, J. Klay
1-3 John : a general reader. – Wilmore, KY : GlossaHouse, ©2013.

    188 pages ; 22 cm. – (Accessible Greek resources and online studies series. Tier 3)

    1 John / J. Klay Harrison – 2-3 John / Chad M. Foster
    ISBN 9780615828541 (paperback)

    1. Bible. Epistles of John – Translating. 2. Bible. Epistles of John – Terminology. 3. Greek language, Biblical – Grammar. 4. Bible. – New Testament – Greek – Language, style.   I. Foster, Chad M. II. Title. III. Series.

BS2805.55.H37 2013   227/.9407

SBLGNT is the *The Greek New Testament: SBL Edition.* Copyright 2010 Society of Biblical Literature and Logos Bible Software [ISBN 978-1-58983-535-1]. The SBLGNT text can be found online at http://sblgnt.com. Information about the "Society of Biblical Literature" can be found at http://sbl-site.org and "Logos Bible Software" at http://logos.com.

The fonts used to create this work are available from linguistsoftware.com/lgku.htm.
Babel Lexicography (BabLex), licensed by J. Klay Harrison and Chad M. Foster, 2012.
Koine Greek Paradigm Chart created by J. Klay Harrison with assistance from Fredrick J. Long.

COVER DESIGN by Asa Harrison.
BOOK DESIGN by Chad M. Foster and J. Klay Harrison.

Contents

AGROS

Accessible Greek Resources and Online Studies

AGROS

The Greek word ἀγρός is a field where seeds are planted and growth occurs. It can also denote a small village or community that forms around such a field. The type of community envisioned here is one that attends to Holy Scripture, particularly one that encourages the use of biblical Greek. Accessible Greek Resources and Online Studies (AGROS) is a tiered curriculum suite featuring innovative readers, grammars, specialized studies, and other exegetical resources to encourage and foster the exegetical use of biblical Greek. The goal of AGROS is to facilitate the creation and publication of innovative and inexpensive print and digital resources for the exposition of Scripture within the context of the global church. The AGROS curriculum includes five tiers, and each tier is indicated on the book's cover: Tier 1 (Beginning I), Tier 2 (Beginning II), Tier 3 (Intermediate I), Tier 4 (Intermediate II), and Tier 5 (Advanced). There are also two resource tracks: Conversational and Translational. Both involve intensive study of morphology, grammar, syntax, and discourse features. The conversational track specifically values the spoken word, and the enhanced learning associated with speaking a language in actual conversation. The translational track values the written word, and encourages analytical study to aide in understanding and translating biblical Greek and other Greek literature. The two resource tracks complement one another and can be pursued independently or together.

ABBREVIATIONS

1st	first person
2nd	second person
3rd	third person
F,ϝ	digamma (Greek letter used up to about 200 BC)
abl.	ablative
abs.	absolute, absolutely
acc.	accusative
act.	active
add.	additional, additionally
adj.	adjective
adv.	adverb, adverbial, adverbially
alt.	alternately
ans.	answer
ante.	antecedent
aor.	aorist
app.	apposition, appositional
art.	article
attrib.	attributive, attributively
aug.	augment
Barclay	Newman, Barclay M., ed. *A Concise Greek-English Dictionary of the New Testament.* Stuttgart: Deutsche Bibelgesellschaft, 1993.
BDAG	Bauer, F., F. W. Danker, et al., eds. *A Greek-English Lexicon of the New Testament and Other Early Christian Literature.* 3rd ed. Chicago: University of Chicago Press, 2000.
beg.	beginning
btw.	between
cmpd.	compound
comp.	comparative, comparatively
conj.	conjunction
constr.	construct, construction.
correl.	correlative
corresp.	corresponding, correspondingly

dat.	dative
dem.	demonstrative
dep.	deponent
diph.	diphtong
dir.	direct
dissim.	dissimilate, dissimilation
ditrans.	ditransitive (trivalent)
ECM	Aland, Barbara, Kurt Aland, Gerd Mink and Klaus Wachtel, eds. *Novum Testamentum Graecum: Editio Critica Maior*, vol. 4: *Catholic Letters*. 4 installments. Stuttgart: Deutsche Biblegesellschaft, 1997–2005.
e.g.	exempli gratia, Latin: "for example"
em.	emendation
emph.	emphatic
encl.	enclitic
equiv.	equivalent
esp.	especially
euphem.	euphemism
fem.	feminine
fig.	figurative, figuratively
fut.	future
gen.	genitive, genitival
GNT	Greek New Testament
GR	General Reader
Greeven	Huck, Albert. *Synopse der drei ersten Evangelien/ Synopsis of the First Three Gospels.* 13th ed. Revised by Heinrich Greeven. Tübingen: Mohr Siebeck, 1981.
hist.	historical
Holmes	Michael W. Holmes
imper.	impersonal (avalent)
impf.	imperfect
impv.	imperative
indef.	indefinite
indic.	indicative
indir.	indirect

inf.	infinitive
init.	initial
instr.	instrumental
inter.	interrogative
intrans.	intransitive (monovalent)
irreg.	irregular
L&N	Louw, Johannes P., and Eugene A. Nida, eds. *Greek-English Lexicon of the New Testament: Based on Semantic Domains*. 2 vols. 2nd ed. New York: United Bible Societies, 1989.
length.	lengthen, lengthened
lit.	literally
loc.	locative
LSJ	Liddell, Henry G., R. Scott, H. S. Jones, and R. McKenzie, eds. *A Greek-English Lexicon*. Rev. 9th ed. Oxford: Clarendon, 1996.
masc.	masculine
mid.	middle
metaph.	metaphor, metaphorical
MH	morphology help
Mounce	Mounce, William D. *The Morphology of Biblical Greek*. Grand Rapids: Zondervan, 1994.
Muraoka	Muraoka, T. *A Greek-English Lexicon of the Septuagint*. Louvain: Peeters, 2009.
neg.	negative, negate(d)
neut.	neuter
nom.	nominative, nominal
NA	Greek text of the NA[27] and UBS[4]
NA[27]	Aland, Barbara, K. Aland, J. Karavidopoulos, C. M. Martini, and B. M. Metzger, eds. *Novum Testamentum Graece*. 27th ed. Stuttgart: Deutsche Bibelgesellschaft, 1993.
NA[28]	Aland, Barbara, K. Aland, J. Karavidopoulos, C. M. Martini, B. M. Metzger, and Institute for New Testament Textual Research, eds. *Novum Testamentum Graece*, 28th ed. Stuttgart: Deutsche Bibelgesellschaft, 2012.

NIV	Goodrich , Richard J., and Albert L. Lukaszewski, eds., *A Reader's Greek New Testament.* Grand Rapids: Zondervan, 2003.
NRSV	New Revised Standard Version
obj.	object
opt.	optative
paren.	parenthetical
pass.	passive
per.	person, personal
periphr.	periphrastic
pf.	perfect, perfective
pl.	plural
plpf.	pluperfect
PN	personal name
pos.	positive
poss.	possessive
post.	postcedent
prec.	preceding
pred.	predicate
pref.	prefix, prefixed
prep.	preposition, prepositional
pres.	present
pron.	pronoun
prtc.	participle
reduc.	reduction
redupl.	reduplicate, reduplication
ref.	reference
reflex.	reflexive
rel.	relative
RP	Robinson, Maurice A., and William G. Pierpont, eds. *The New Testament in the Original Greek: Byzantine Textform 2005.* Southborough, Mass.: Chilton, 2005.
SBL	Society of Biblical Literature
SBLGNT	Holmes, Michael W. *The Greek New Testament: SBL Edition.* Atlanta: Society of Biblical Literature, 2010. http://sblgnt.com/.

SBLGNT[app]	Apparatus of SBLGNT
sg.	singular
Smyth	Smyth, Herbert Weir. *Greek Grammar*. Revised by Gordon M. Messing. Cambridge, Mass.: Harvard University Press, 1984.
subj.	subjunctive
subst.	substantival, substantive
suf.	suffix, suffixed
superl.	superlative
suppl.	suppletive
syn.	synonym
TDNT	Friedrich, Gerhard, and Gerhard Kittel, eds. *Theological Dictionary of the New Testament*. 10 vols., tr. by G. W. Bromiley. Grand Rapids, Mich.: Eerdmans, 1964–76.
TH	Translation Help
TLNT	Spicq, Ceslas. *Theological Lexicon of the New Testament*. 3 vols. Peabody, Mass.: Hendrickson, 1994.
TR	Textus Receptus ("Received Text")
trans.	transitive (divalent)
translit.	transliteration (of a loan word into Greek)
Treg	Tregelles, Samuel Prideaux. *The Greek New Testament, Edited from Ancient Authorities, with their Various Readings in Full, and the Latin Version of Jerome*. London: Bagster; Stewart, 1857–1879.
Treg[marg]	margin of Treg
Trenchard	Trenchard, Warren C. *Complete Vocabulary Guide to the Greek New Testament*. Rev. ed. Grand Rapids, Mich.: Zondervan, 1998.
UBS[4]	Aland, B., K. Aland, J. Karavidopoulos, C. M. Martini, and B. M. Metzger, eds. *The Greek New Testament*. 4th rev. ed. New York: United Bible Societies, 2006.
voc.	vocative

WH   Hort, Fenton John Anthony, and Brooke Foss
                     Westcott. *The New Testament in the Original*
                     Greek. 2 vols. Cambridge: Macmillan, 1881.

WH[app]   *Appendix* (vol. 2 of WH)

WH[marg]   margin of WH

Works (TJ)   Jackson, Thomas, ed. *The Works of the Rev. John*
                     Wesley, M.A. 14 vols. Grand Rapids: Baker,
                     1978.

PREFACE TO THE GENERAL READERS

*And men who speak the Latin tongue, of whom are those
I have undertaken to instruct, need two other languages
for the knowledge of Scripture, Hebrew and Greek, that
they may have recourse to the original texts if the endless
diversity of the Latin translators throw them into doubt.*

— Saint Augustine, *De Doctrina Christiana* 2.11.16

*Do I understand Greek and Hebrew? Otherwise, how can
I undertake, (as every Minister does,) not only to explain
books which are written therein, but to defend them against
all opponents? Am I not at the mercy of everyone who does
understand, or even pretends to understand, the original?
For which way can I confute his pretense? Do I understand
the language of the Old Testament? critically? at all? Can
I read into English one of David's Psalms, or even the first
chapter of Genesis? Do I understand the language of the
New Testament? Am I a critical master of it? Have I enough
of it even to read into English the first chapter of St. Luke?
If not, how many years did I spend at school? How many
at the University? And what was I doing all those years?
Ought not shame to cover my face?*

— John Wesley, "An Address to the Clergy," *Works* (TJ) X:491.

Learning Koinē Greek can be a daunting task. Some students
learn just enough to fulfill degree requirements and then
forget most of what they learned. This is a sad fact, especially
since many people would love such an opportunity to read
Scripture in the original languages. Forgetting Greek may not
be intentional, yet it is a reality for numerous students. While
many resources are available that teach the grammatical basics
of Koinē Greek, the beginning student is often still not able to
read their Greek New Testament (GNT). Beginning students
are often hindered from reading the GNT due to a lack of
vocabulary or unfamiliarity with Koinē Greek syntax and
idioms.

1

A *General Reader* of the Greek New Testament is a Tier 3 resource that assumes the completion of beginning Greek instruction. It is designed to build confidence and encourage the reading of the GNT by providing vocabulary glosses, morphological explanations, and translation helps, while also assisting the student to transition from beginning into intermediate Greek studies. By carefully working through the *General Reader*, students will find value interacting with the GNT and see how grammatical classifications affect meaning and translation in context.

Any student who uses A *General Reader* of the Greek New Testament will be able to apply her/his beginning Greek education and read from the GNT. By doing so, it is hoped that the GNT might become a part of daily reading and proclamation. Interpreters, pastors, and students will find the *General Reader* beneficial for careful investigation of the GNT.

J. Klay Harrison
May 2013

How to Use the General Reader

A *General Reader* of the Greek New Testament is designed to be a user-friendly guide for reading the GNT. The *General Reader* (GR) will provide footnotes with morphological and textual helps, variants between the SBLGNT and the standard critical editions of the GNT, and all vocabulary that occurs 49 times or less. Additionally, each chapter is introduced with a vocabulary list of these infrequent words that occur within the chapter. The list is sorted by word frequency as found in the chapter, arranged from most to least frequent.

The Greek Text

The main Greek text of the GR is *The Greek New Testament: SBL Edition* (SBLGNT). This edition is a critical text of the GNT and includes a text-critical apparatus. The SBLGNT text and apparatus are explained in the "Introduction to the SBLGNT," which follows this section. The "Introduction to the SBLGNT" expounds not only how the SBLGNT text was assembled but also how to use the text-critical apparatus found in Appendix I. The introduction was written by Michael Holmes and is also found in *The Greek New Testament: SBL Edition*.

> SBLGNT is the *The Greek New Testament: SBL Edition*. Copyright 2010 Society of Biblical Literature and Logos Bible Software [ISBN 978-1-58983-535-1]. The SBLGNT text can be found online at http://sblgnt. com. Information about the "Society of Biblical Literature" can be found at http://sbl-site.org and "Logos Bible Software" at http://logos.com.

THE TEXT-CRITICAL APPARATUS

The text-critical markings found in the SBLGNT point the reader to the apparatus, which is included in Appendix I of the GR. For an explanation of the text critical marks and the apparatus, please see "Introduction to the SBLGNT."

THE FOOTNOTES

For ease of reading, the GR uses footnotes as a guide through the GNT. The footnotes provide four categories of information; 1) lexical aid, 2) morphology help (MH), 3) translation help (TH), and 4) NA (NA^{27}/UBS^4) and NA^{28} variants. Each category is described below.

1. If a Greek word occurs 49 times or less in the SBLGNT, then lexical aid is provided in a footnote. Each Greek word is provided in lexical (dictionary) form. Thus, all verbs are presented in **pres. act. indic. 1st sg.** conjugation. Pronouns and adjectives are shown in **nom. sg. masc.** form followed by the **nom. sg. fem.** and **nom. sg. neut.** endings. The lexical form for a noun is the **nom. sg.** full inflection followed by the **gen. sg.** ending and then the respective article, which indicates gender. After the word's lexical form, glosses are found in italics. These glosses are general meanings for the Greek word, so they are not comprehensive of the word's complete lexical range. Since words only have meaning in context, there are times when a standard gloss is not appropriate for adequate translation. In these instances, a contextual gloss will be suggested in a bold italic font following a semicolon, e.g.,

1 λόγος, ου, ὁ, *word, speech, matter;* ***concept.***

In this example, the Greek word in question is a form of λόγος. Since λόγος is a noun, the fully inflected nom. sg. masc. form (λόγος) is provided. Then follows the gen. ending (ου), which lets the reader know this is a 2ⁿᵈ declension noun. The article (ὁ) is given in nom. sg. masc. inflected form. Since ὁ is masc., the article then indicates λόγος is a masc. noun. Thus, the entire lexical form is λόγος, ου, ὁ. Then, to translate λόγος, the GR suggests using one of the following standard glosses: *word, speech, matter*. However, it appears these standard glosses do not capture the true meaning of λόγος within the given context. So, the GR also provides a contextual gloss to better fit this particular context. Thus, here it is suggested that λόγος should be translated as ***concept***.

2. Morphology Help (MH) is also provided in the footnotes. These notes supply potentially difficult parsing, explain word formation, and clarify any morphological issues, e.g.,

> 2 MH: fut. act. indic. 2ⁿᵈ pl. from μένω = μεν (root) + εσ (tense formative) + ετε (thematic 2ⁿᵈ pl. ending) › μεν + εετε (σ btw. two vowels elides) › μενεῖτε (vowels contract; ε + ε = εῖ).

The initials MH in this footnote denotes the following as morphology help. The particular word in question is μενεῖτε. The parsing is given along with the lexical form. Then a detailed explanation shows step by step how the inflected verb was formed.

3. The third footnote category is the Translation Help (TH), which provides brief explanations for difficult grammar, idioms, morphology, and syntax, e.g.,

> 3 TH: λόγου is dir.obj. of ἀκούει.

The initials TH in the footnote illustration marks what follows as a translation help. λόγου is the word in question within the main Greek text. The TH is telling the reader that, in this clause, λόγου is functioning as the direct object of the verb ἀκούει.

Students should be aware that at times certain phrases will be placed in front of the verb for various reasons. Though it is beyond the purpose of this GR to discuss prominence and emphasis, there will be some Translation Helps marking the Greek wordage as "fronted."

4. Any difference in spelling between the SBLGNT, NA, and NA[28] are also available in a footnote. This will be evidenced by "NA has" (or "NA[28] has") and then the textual difference. Although some of these variants are presented in the text-critical apparatus found in the Appendix I, they are included in the footnotes for sake of quick reference, e.g.,

4   NA has ῥῆμα.

Here the footnote informs the reader that the NA Greek texts have ῥῆμα where the SBLGNT has something different.

THE VOCABULARY AND GLOSSES

The beginning Koinē Greek student should learn every word that occurs in the GNT 50 times or more (310 words). The GR includes glosses for these high frequency words in Appendices II and III. They are listed both by frequency (for vocabulary retention) and in alphabetical order (for quick reference). Every word that occurs 49 times or less in the SBLGNT will be glossed in the footnote section of the GR. Additionally, each chapter is introduced with a vocabulary list of these glossed words that occur within the chapter. The list is sorted by word frequency as found in the chapter, arranged from most to least frequent in the SBLGNT. All word frequencies are based upon lexical occurrences in the SBLGNT, not the NA or NA[28].

The goal in establishing vocabulary glosses is to provide accurate yet concise glosses for every word. Knowing that words only have meaning in context, standard glosses will not suffice for every word occurrence. Such is the limit of a gloss. Whenever a standard glosses does not fix the context, a contextual gloss will be available in a footnote.

All glosses are a collaborative effort between the author(s), AGROS Editorial Board, and Babel Lexicography (BabLex). These glosses are the result of independent research and the consultation of numerous resources, which include but are not limited to: Barclay, BDAG, Muraoka, LSJ, L&N, TDNT, TLNT, and Trenchard.

THE APPENDICES

The GR appendices include four sections: Appendix I: SBLGNT Apparatus, Appendix II: Vocabulary 50 times or more sorted by frequency, Appendix III: Vocabulary 50 times or more arranged alphabetically, and Appendix IV: Koinē Greek Paradigm Charts. Each appendix is described below.

Appendix I: SBLGNT Apparatus. Throughout the Greek text, text-critical marks will point the reader to the SBLGNT Apparatus (SBLGNT^app). This apparatus has been placed in Appendix I. For an explanation of the text-critical marks and how to use the SBLGNT^app, please see the section entitled "Introduction to the SBLGNT."

The General Readers for the Catholic Letters (James, 1–2 Peter, 1–3 John, and Jude) will include an additional apparatus at the end of Appendix I that shows any differences between the SBLGNT and ECM (*Novum Testamentum Graecum: Editio Critica Maior*). This short apparatus is from the SBLGNT, which is there titled "Appendix: The SBLGNT in comparison to ECM."

Appendix II: Vocabulary 50 times or more sorted by frequency. In order to best serve the Koinē Greek student, all vocabulary assumed as known has been sorted from most to least frequent and is included in Appendix II. The frequency of occurance for each word is based upon the SBLGNT and not the NA. These 310 words, which occur 50 times or more in the SBLGNT, are available for students wanting to learn or refresh their basic Greek vocabulary.

Appendix III: Vocabulary 50 times or more arranged alphabetically. All vocabulary occurring 50 times or more in the SBLGNT, which is assumed as known, is arranged alphabetically in Appendix III.

Appendix IV: Koinē Greek Paradigm Charts. These paradigm charts will be a helpful resource to students having difficulty parsing words or just needing a quick reminder about Greek endings. The *Koinē Greek Paradigm Charts* were created by J. Klay Harrison with assistance from Fredrick J. Long.

Introduction to the SBLGNT[1]

The Text

The *SBL Greek New Testament* (SBLGNT) is a new edition of the Greek New Testament, established with the help of earlier editions. In particular, four editions of the Greek New Testament were utilized as primary resources in the process of establishing the SBLGNT. These editions (and their abbreviations) are:

WH   Brooke Foss Westcott and Fenton John Anthony Hort, *The New Testament in the Original Greek*, vol. 1: *Text*; vol. 2: *Introduction* [and] *Appendix* (Cambridge: Macmillan, 1881). This justly famous and widely influential nineteenth-century edition of the Greek New Testament was one of the key texts used in the creation of the original Nestle text[2] and was used as the initial basis of comparison in the creation of the United Bible Societies' *Greek New Testament*.[3]

Treg   Samuel Prideaux Tregelles, *The Greek New Testament, Edited from Ancient Authorities, with their Various Readings in Full, and the Latin Version of Jerome* (London: Bagster; Stewart, 1857–1879).

---

1 This introduction is a reproduction of the existing introduction written by Michael W. Holmes in the SBLGNT.

2 Eberhard Nestle, *Novum Testamentum Graece* (Stuttgart: Württembergische Bibelanstalt, 1898); cf. the 16th ed. (1936), 38*; cf. also Kurt Aland and Barbara Aland, *The Text of the New Testament* (2nd ed.; trans. E. F. Rhodes; Grand Rapids: Eerdmans; Leiden: Brill, 1989), 19–20.

3 Kurt Aland, Matthew Black, Bruce M. Metzger, and Allen Wikgren, eds., *The Greek New Testament* (New York: American Bible Society; London: British and Foreign Bible Society; Edinburgh: National Bible Society of Scotland; Amsterdam: Netherlands Bible Society; Stuttgart: Württemberg Bible Society, 1966), v.

Although the fine edition of Tregelles has been overshadowed by that of his close contemporaries Westcott and Hort, his textual judgments reveal a "consistency of view and breadth of appreciation" of all the available textual evidence not always as evident in the work of his major nineteenth-century colleagues, who display (to varying degrees) a tendency toward a preoccupation with the latest "big discovery" (Ephraemi Rescriptus/04 in the case of Lachmann, Sinaiticus/01 in the case of Tischendorf, and Vaticanus/03 in the case of Westcott and Hort).[4] Tregelles offers a discerning alternative perspective alongside Westcott and Hort.

NIV   Richard J. Goodrich and Albert L. Lukaszewski, *A Reader's Greek New Testament* (Grand Rapids: Zondervan, 2003). This edition presents the Greek text behind the New International Version[5] as reconstructed by Edward Goodrick and John Kohlenberger III.[6] It thus represents the textual choices made by the Committee on Bible Translation, the international group of scholars responsible for the NIV translation. According to its editors, this edition differs from the United Bible Societies/Nestle-Aland editions of the Greek New Testament at 231 places.[7]

RP   *The New Testament in the Original Greek: Byzantine Textform 2005*, compiled and arranged by Maurice A.

---

4 David C. Parker, "The Development of the Critical Text of the Epistle of James: From Lachmann to the *Editio Critica Maior*," in *New Testament Textual Criticism and Exegesis: Festschrift J. Delobel* (ed. A. Denaux; BETL 161; Leuven: Leuven University Press and Peeters, 2002), 329.

5 *The Holy Bible, New International Version: New Testament* (Grand Rapids: Zondervan, 1973).

6 A second edition published by the same editors and publisher in 2007 (reviewed and modified by Gordon Fee) presents the Greek text behind the TNIV translation.

7 Goodrich and Lukaszewski, *A Reader's Greek New Testament*, 10 n. 6.

Robinson and William G. Pierpont (Southborough, Mass.: Chilton, 2005). This edition offers a text that is a reliable representative of the Byzantine textual tradition.

ESTABLISHING THE TEXT

The starting point for the SBLGNT was the edition of Westcott and Hort. First, the WH text was modified to match the orthographic standards of the SBLGNT (described below). Next, the modified version was compared to the other three primary editions (Treg, NIV, and RP) in order to identify points of agreement and disagreement between them. Where all four editions agreed, the text was tentatively accepted as the text of the SBL edition; points of disagreement were marked for further consideration. The editor then worked systematically through the entire text, giving particular attention to the points of disagreement but examining as well the text where all four editions were in agreement.[8] Where there was disagreement among the four editions, the editor determined which variant to print as the text;[9] occasionally a reading not found in any of the four editions commended itself as the most probable representative of the text and therefore was adopted. Similarly, where all four texts were in agreement, the editor determined whether to accept that reading or to adopt an alternative variant as the text.[10] In this manner, the text of the SBLGNT was established.

---

8 For a brief overview of the editor's methodological and historical perspectives with regard to the practice of New Testament textual criticism, see Michael W. Holmes, "Reconstructing the Text of the New Testament," in *The Blackwell Companion to the New Testament* (ed. David E. Aune; Oxford: Wiley-Blackwell, 2010), 77–89.

9 Or, to put the matter a bit more precisely, which variant most likely represents the form in which the text first began to be copied and to circulate.

10 In all, there are fifty-six variation units in the SBLGNT where the editor preferred a reading not found in any of the four primary editions. In thirty-eight of those instances, the editor's preferred reading is also read by WHmarg (30x) and/or Tregmarg (2x) and/or NA (10x).

A comparison of this new text with the four editions listed above, using as the database the 6,928 variation units recorded in the accompanying apparatus (described below), reveals the following patterns of agreement and difference:

	Agreements	Disagreements
SBL—WH:	6,047	881
SBL—Treg:	5,699	1,229
SBL—NIV:	6,310	618
SBL—RP:	970	5,958

Also interesting is a comparison of agreements of the SBLGNT with one of the four editions against the other three and, vice versa, SBLGNT and the other three against the one:

SBL + WH vs. Treg NIV RP: 99   SBL + Treg NIV RP vs. WH: 365

SBL + Treg vs. WH NIV RP: 28   SBL + WH NIV RP vs. Treg: 150

SBL + NIV vs. WH Treg RP: 59   SBL + WH Treg RP vs. NIV: 103

SBL + RP vs. WH Treg NIV: 66   SBL + WH Treg NIV vs. RP: 4,874

ORTHOGRAPHY AND RELATED MATTERS

The orthography of this edition (including accents and breathings[11]) follows that of the Bauer-Danker-Arndt-Gingrich lexicon (BDAG).[12] This includes both text and apparatus:

---

11   Occasionally breathings are as much a matter of interpretation as of lexicography. In agreement with a minority of the membership of the UBS Editorial Committee (see Bruce M. Metzger, *A Textual Commentary on The Greek New Testament* [London: United Bible Societies, 1971], 616 [a discussion of Phil 3:21 not found in the second edition]), the SBLGNT occasionally prints a rough breathing on forms of αὐτός.

12   *A Greek-English Lexicon of the New Testament and Other*

entries in the apparatus generally have been conformed to the orthography of BDAG regardless of the spelling of the source edition.

With regard to elision (e.g., ἀλλ' for ἀλλά), crasis (e.g., κἀγώ for καὶ ἐγώ), movable ν, and the interchange between first aorist and second aorist verb endings, the text of Westcott and Hort has been followed. As in the case of orthography, this guideline generally applies to the apparatus as well as the text.

CAPITALIZATION

Capitalization follows the pattern of the third edition of *The Apostolic Fathers: Greek Texts and English Translations*,[13] which capitalizes (1) the first word of a paragraph; (2) the first word of direct speech; and (3) proper nouns.[14] Occasionally capitalization in a variant reading in the apparatus may follow that of the source edition.

Early Christian Literature (3rd ed., revised and edited by Frederick William Danker; based on the 6th ed. of Walter Bauer's *Griechisch-deutsches Wörterbuch zu den Schriften des Neuen Testaments und der frühchristlichen Literatur*; Chicago: University of Chicago Press, 2000). Thus ἁγνεία, not ἁγνία (so WH), or, e.g., in the case of words with movable ς (cf. BDF §21), ἄχρι, μέχρι, and οὕτως are printed throughout, unless BDAG indicates otherwise (ἄχρις, Gal 3:19 and Heb 3:13; μέχρις, Mark 13:30, Gal 4:19, Heb 12:4; οὕτω, Acts 23:11, Phil 3:17, Heb 12:21, Rev 16:18). A rare exception to the guideline is the adoption of νουμηνίας rather than νεομηνίας in Col 2:16.

13 Michael W. Holmes, ed., *The Apostolic Fathers: Greek Texts and English Translations* (3rd ed.; Grand Rapids: Baker Academic, 2007).

14 A category that offers, to be sure, numerous opportunities for differences of opinion.

Verse Division, Punctuation, and Paragraphing

The verse divisions follow those of the Nestle-Aland/United Bible Societies Greek texts throughout.[15] Differences between editions have not been recorded.

Punctuation generally follows that of Westcott and Hort. Regular exceptions include instances where a textual decision or the adoption of NRSV paragraphing required a corresponding change in punctuation. Where Westcott and Hort employed two consecutive punctuation marks (such as a comma following or preceding a dash; see 1 Tim 1:5, 2:7), these have been reduced to a single mark. A high point has been added before direct speech if no other punctuation is present. Occasionally other changes have been made as required by context.

Paragraphing generally follows the pattern of the NRSV. Conflicts between NRSV paragraphing and Westcott and Hort punctuation have been resolved on a contextual basis.[16]

Symbols used in the Text

⌐ or ⌐ or ⌐˙   A textual note pertains to the following word. When identical words in the same verse are marked, the dotted bracket designates the second occurrence. Third (and subsequent) instances are denoted by a numbered bracket to distinguish them from previous instances.

( ) or (˙)   A textual note pertains to the enclosed words.

---

15 A partial exception occurs at the end of Acts 19, where (in accordance with some editions and many recent translations) a forty-first verse number has been placed in the text, but in brackets ([41]), to indicate uncertainty regarding its status.

16 For example, at the end of Phil 1:18, WH's punctuation was given preference over the NRSV paragraph break, whereas at Phil 2:14 the NRSV paragraphing was followed rather than the WH punctuation (which was changed accordingly).

When identical phrases in the same verse are marked, dotted brackets designate the second occurrence. Similarly, when a second multiword variation unit falls within the boundaries of a longer multiword variation unit, the dotted brackets mark the second occurrence.

[ ]   The enclosed text is doubtful.[17]

THE APPARATUS

The textual apparatus provides information about a wide range of textual variants.[18] It records all differences between the text of the SBLGNT and the texts of WH, Treg, NIV, RP, and NA except for those differences that fall in the category of "orthography and related matters" (discussed above).[19] That is,

---

17 Brackets have been employed in this edition sparingly—not, one hopes, due to a lack of what Parker nicely terms "wise reticence" in the face of difficult choices (Parker, "Development," 325), but for positive reasons. These include a widely shared sense that brackets have been somewhat overused in some recent editions (sometimes as what could be perceived as a means of avoiding difficult choices); an opinion that one of an editor's duties is to make choices, particularly in the "hard cases," so as to offer some degree of guidance to those making use of the resulting text; and a corresponding concern that the availability of brackets biases the decision-making process toward inclusion (one can bracket an included word about which one has some degree of doubt regarding the decision to include it, but one cannot bracket the omission of a word about which one has an equal degree of doubt regarding the decision to exclude it). In all, for better or worse, single brackets appear only six times in the SBLGNT (at Luke 22:19–20; 24:40; 24:51; 24:52; Eph 1:1; Col 1:20).

18 In general, it closely follows the pattern of the apparatus in Holmes, *The Apostolic Fathers* (3rd ed.).

19 This means that the apparatus includes nearly all the variant or alternative readings noted in the margins or notes of most recent major English translations and numerous translations into other languages as well.

the apparatus does not take note of differences that are solely a matter of orthographic variation or that involve only elision, crasis, movable ν, interchange between first and second aorist verb endings, and the like; it does record all other differences between the SBL text and the texts of the five other editions just listed.

The four primary editions (WH Treg NIV RP) are cited for every variation unit (of which there are 6,928).[20] NA is cited only when it differs from NIV. Occasionally a marginal reading of WH or Treg or the text of another edition is cited, usually in support of a reading adopted by the editor that is not found in any of the four primary editions, but sometimes in other circumstances as well.

In each note, the reading of the text is always presented first, in bold, followed by its supporting evidence; the variant reading(s) and supporting evidence follow. Because the different editions use single brackets ([ ]) in the text in different ways, the apparatus does not record details regarding an edition's use of brackets in its text.

SYMBOLS USED IN THE NOTES

•	Separates multiple variation units within a verse.
]	Separates the reading of the text (and its support) from variant readings.
;	Separates multiple variants within a single variation unit.
+	The following text is added by the listed witness(es).

---

20 For variants involving the verses or parts of verses that WH print between double brackets (⟦ ⟧), WH is cited in the apparatus between brackets (i.e., ⟦WH⟧).

–   The indicated text is omitted by the listed
                           witness(es).

⟦ ⟧   Used by Westcott and Hort to mark material
                           that they did not think belonged to the
                           genuine text but that they did not feel free
                           to remove completely from their printed text
                           due to its antiquity or intrinsic interest. When
                           placed around their initials in the apparatus
                           (i.e., ⟦WH⟧), double brackets signal that
                           WH placed them around the text or variant
                           reading in question.

...   Replaces identical text shared by all the
                           variants in a particular variation unit.

ABBREVIATIONS USED IN THE NOTES

ECM   *Novum Testamentum Graecum: Editio
                           Critica Maior*, ed. The Institute for New
                           Testament Textual Research, vol. 4: *Catholic
                           Letters*, ed. Barbara Aland, Kurt Aland,
                           Gerd Mink, Holger Strutwolf, and Klaus
                           Wachtel (4 installments; Stuttgart: Deutsche
                           Biblegesellschaft, 1997–2005): inst. 1: *James*
                           (1997; 2nd rev. impr., 1998); inst. 2: *The
                           Letters of Peter* (2000); inst. 3: *The First
                           Letter of John* (2003); inst. 4: *The Second
                           and Third Letter of John, The Letter of Jude*
                           (2005).

em   emendation

Greeven   Indicates a reading printed as the text by
                           Heinrich Greeven in Albert Huck, *Synopse
                           der drei ersten Evangelien/Synopsis of the*

First Three Gospels (13th ed. fundamentally revised by Heinrich Greeven; Tübingen: Mohr Siebeck), 1981).

Holmes · Indicates a reading preferred by the editor that is not found in any of the four primary editions.

NA · Represents the NA$^{26-27}$/UBS$^{3-4}$ editions, which all print the identical Greek text. NA is explicitly cited only when it differs from NIV.

NIV · Richard J. Goodrich and Albert L. Lukaszewski, eds., *A Reader's Greek New Testament* (Grand Rapids: Zondervan, 2003).

RP · *The New Testament in the Original Greek: Byzantine Textform 2005*, compiled and arranged by Maurice A. Robinson and William G. Pierpont (Southborough, Mass.: Chilton, 2005).

TR · *Textus Receptus* ("Received Text"). The phrase technically designates the edition of the Greek New Testament printed by the Elziver Brothers in 1633; in generic use it can designate not only the Elziver text but also its precursors (Erasmus, Stephanus, and Beza) or any similar text.[21]

Treg · Samuel Prideaux Tregelles, *The Greek New Testament, Edited from Ancient Authorities,*

---

21 For example, F. H. A. Scrivener, ed., *Η ΚΑΙΝΗ ΔΙΑΘΗΚΗ, Novum Testamentum: Textus Stephanici* A.D. *1550* (4th ed., corrected by E. Nestle; London: Bell; Cambridge: Deighton, Bell, 1906) (the printing of the TR consulted for this edition).

with their Various Readings in Full, and the Latin Version of Jerome (London: Bagster; Stewart, 1857–1879).

Treg^{marg}	Indicates a reading printed by Tregelles in the margin of his edition.

Treg^{marg}   Indicates a reading printed by Tregelles in the margin of his edition.

WH   Brooke Foss Westcott and Fenton John Anthony Hort, *The New Testament in the Original Greek,* vol. 1: *Text*; vol. 2: *Introduction* [and] *Appendix* (Cambridge: Macmillan, 1881).

WH^{app}   Indicates a reading discussed by WH in the *Appendix* to their edition (in vol. 2).

WH^{marg}   Indicates an alternative reading printed by WH in the margin of their edition.

UNDERSTANDING THE APPARATUS: A BRIEF GUIDE

This brief guide supplements what is said above about the apparatus to the SBLGNT by offering further explanation and examples.

The textual apparatus provides a textual note for each of the more than 6,900 instances of variation in the SBLGNT. In each note, the marked reading in the text is always listed first, in bold, and followed immediately by its supporting evidence. The separator bracket (]) comes next, followed by the variant reading(s) and supporting evidence. Multiple variation units in the same verse are separated by a bullet (•), as in all three examples below. Multiple variant readings in the same variation unit are separated by a semicolon (;), as in the second variant in Matt 22:30 below (τοῦ θεοῦ RP; – WH Treg NIV).

Symbols in the text alert the reader to the presence of textual notes in the apparatus. The most frequently used symbols are ⌐ and ⸄ ⸅; the former marks a single word, and the latter encloses a multiple word phrase. If the same word is marked a second time in the same verse, the ⌐ symbol is used to mark the second occurrence (as in Matt 10:28 below, twice). If an identical multiword phrase is marked a second time in the same verse, the ⸄ ⸅ symbols are used to mark the second occurrence (as in John 18:39 below). In both cases, for clarity the symbols are repeated in the textual note. (More complex cases are discussed below.)

Matt 10:28 text:

> 28 καὶ μὴ ⌐φοβεῖσθε ἀπὸ τῶν ἀποκτεννόντων τὸ σῶμα τὴν δὲ ψυχὴν μὴ δυναμένων ἀποκτεῖναι· ⌐φοβεῖσθε δὲ μᾶλλον τὸν δυνάμενον ⌐καὶ ψυχὴν ⌐καὶ σῶμα ἀπολέσαι ἐν γεέννῃ.

textual note in apparatus:

28 ⌐φοβεῖσθε Treg NIV RP] φοβηθῆτε WH
• ⌐**φοβεῖσθε** WH NIV] φοβήθητε Treg RP
• ⌐**καὶ** WH Treg NIV] + τὴν RP • ⌐**καὶ** WH Treg NIV] + τὸ RP

John 18:39 text:

> 39 ἔστιν δὲ συνήθεια ὑμῖν ἵνα ἕνα ⸄ἀπολύσω ὑμῖν⸅ ἐν τῷ πάσχα· βούλεσθε οὖν ⸄ἀπολύσω ὑμῖν⸅ τὸν βασιλέα τῶν Ἰουδαίων;

textual note in apparatus:

39 ⸄ἀπολύσω ὑμῖν⸅ WH Treg NIV] ὑμῖν ἀπολύσω RP • ⸄**ἀπολύσω ὑμῖν**⸅ WH Treg NIV] ὑμῖν ἀπολύσω RP

Matt 22:30 text:

30 ἐν γὰρ τῇ ἀναστάσει οὔτε γαμοῦσιν οὔτε
ᴦγαμίζονται, ἀλλ᾽ ὡς ἄγγελοι ᴦθεοῦ ἐν ᴦτῷ οὐρανῷ
εἰσιν·

textual note in apparatus:

30 γαμίζονται WH Treg NIV] ἐκγαμίζονται
RP • **θεοῦ** Holmes] τοῦ θεοῦ RP; – WH Treg NIV
• **τῷ** WH Treg NIV] – RP

Variant readings can be one of three types: addition,
omission, or substitution. An addition is signaled by the plus
sign (+), which indicates that the following word or words are
added to the reading of the text by the supporting edition(s)
listed after the additional words. In Matt 10:28 above, for
example, taking the third and fourth variants together, the SBL
text reads καὶ ψυχὴν καὶ σῶμα (with WH Treg NIV), while
the RP text—adding τὴν after ᴦκαὶ and τὸ after ᴦκαὶ —reads
καὶ τὴν ψυχὴν καὶ τὸ σῶμα.

An omission is signaled by the minus sign (–) or dash,
which indicates that the word(s) marked in the text are omitted
by the supporting edition(s) listed after the minus sign. In the
second variant in Matt 22:30 above, where the SBL text reads
ὡς ἄγγελοι θεοῦ, WH Treg NIV omit the word θεοῦ, and thus
read only ὡς ἄγγελοι (see also the last variant in 22:30).

If there is neither a plus nor a minus sign, the variant
reading is a substitution: the word(s) marked in the text are
replaced by the word(s) in the variant reading by the supporting
edition(s) listed after the variant reading. In the first variant in
Matt 10:28, for example, the SBL text reads φοβεῖσθε (with
Treg NIV RP), while the WH text reads φοβηθῆτε (see also
the second variant in this verse, both variants in John 18:39,
and the first variant in 22:30).

The above examples cover a very large proportion of the
variation units in the apparatus, though more complex cases

do sometimes occur. If, for example, the same word is marked more than twice in the same sentence, the symbols ⌐1 and ⌐2 are used for subsequent occurrences (as in 1 Cor 12:10 below, where the same word is marked four times). Occasionally, the ⌐ ⌐ symbols (whose typical use was described above) can also be used to mark a shorter multiword variant that occurs inside a longer multiword variant (see Luke 22:43–44 below). Also, a single-word variant marker (⌐) can occur inside a regular set (⌐ ⌐) of multiple-word variant markers (as in John 13:2 below). A key point to remember when encountering an "opening" multiple-word marker, whether ⌐ or ⌐, is to always look for the corresponding "closing" marker (⌐ or ⌐); this will help to avoid confusion.

1 Cor 12:10 text:

> 10 ⌐ἄλλῳ ἐνεργήματα δυνάμεων, ⌐ἄλλῳ προφητεία, ⌐1ἄλλῳ διακρίσεις πνευμάτων, ⌐ἑτέρῳ γένη γλωσσῶν, ⌐2ἄλλῳ ἑρμηνεία γλωσσῶν·

textual note in apparatus:

> 10 ⌐ἄλλῳ Holmes] + δὲ WH Treg NIV RP • ⌐ἄλλῳ Treg] + δὲ WH NIV RP • ⌐1ἄλλῳ Treg] + δὲ WH NIV RP • ἑτέρῳ WH Treg NIV] + δὲ RP • ⌐2ἄλλῳ Holmes] + δὲ WH Treg NIV RP

Luke 22.43–44 text:

> 43 ⌐ὤφθη δὲ αὐτῷ ἄγγελος ⌐ἀπ᾿ οὐρανοῦ ἐνισχύων αὐτόν. 44 καὶ γενόμενος ἐν ἀγωνίᾳ ἐκτενέστερον προσηύχετο· ⌐καὶ ἐγένετο⌐ ὁ ἱδρὼς αὐτοῦ ὡσεὶ θρόμβοι αἵματος καταβαίνοντες ἐπὶ τὴν γῆν.⌐

textual note in apparatus:

43–44 ὤφθη δὲ ... ἐπὶ τὴν γῆν. Treg NIV
RP] ⟦WH⟧ • ἀπ' NIV RP] ἀπὸ τοῦ ⟦WH⟧ Treg
• καὶ ἐγένετο ⟦WH⟧ NIV] ἐγένετο δὲ Treg RP

Here the symbols ⌐ ¬ mark off a variant involving the inclusion (by Treg NIV RP) or omission (by WH) of verses 43–44. Within that larger variant, a smaller multiword variant marked by ⌐ ¬ involves a word-order difference. Since the ⌐ "opening" symbol always is matched by a ¬ "closing" symbol, and the ⌐ symbol always corresponds with ¬, it is possible to "nest" the two variants without confusion as to where each begins and ends. This variant offers an opportunity to comment on the use of another symbol, ⟦WH⟧. There are some verses that Westcott and Hort did not think belonged to the genuine text but that they did not feel free to remove completely from their printed text due to its antiquity or intrinsic interest. In the first entry in the apparatus (**ὤφθη δὲ ... ἐπὶ τὴν γῆν.** Treg NIV RP] ⟦WH⟧), the symbol ⟦WH⟧ signals that Westcott and Hort placed verses 43–44 inside double brackets, whereas Treg NIV RP included them in their texts. In the third variant (**καὶ ἐγένετο** ⟦WH⟧ NIV] ἐγένετο δὲ Treg RP), involving a difference in word order, the presence of ⟦WH⟧ signals that Westcott and Hort support the same word order as NIV and reminds us that they did not view the phrase (or the verse of which it is a part) as part of the original text.

John 13.2 text:

2 καὶ δείπνου ⌐γινομένου, τοῦ διαβόλου ἤδη βεβληκότος εἰς τὴν καρδίαν ⌐ἵνα παραδοῖ αὐτὸν Ἰούδας Σίμωνος ⌐¬Ἰσκαριώτου¬,

textual note in apparatus:

2 **γινομένου** WH Treg NIV] γενομένου RP
• **ἵνα παραδοῖ αὐτὸν Ἰούδας Σίμωνος Ἰσκ.**
WH Treg NIV] Ἰούδα Σίμωνος Ἰσκ. ἵνα αὐτὸν
παραδῷ RP • **Ἰσκαριώτου** NIV RP] Ἰσκαριώτης
WH Treg

In this instance, the word-order variation (ἵνα παραδοῖ αὐτὸν Ἰούδας Σίμωνος Ἰσκαριώτου⸃) is unrelated to the separate variant involving the spelling of ⸀Ἰσκαριώτου, so they have been set up as separate variants, the smaller one "nested" inside the larger. The larger variant bounded by the symbols ⸂ ⸃ deals with the word-order variation, while the variant signaled by the ⸀ symbol deals with the spelling variation.

Two other matters call for comment. One is punctuation, which in general is not taken into account in the textual notes. Occasionally, however, a variant may carry with it consequences for how the verse is punctuated. In these cases, punctuation is included in the textual note, as in the second variant in Rev 21:4:

4 **ἐκ** WH Treg NIV] ἀπὸ RP • **ἔτι.** WH] ἔτι, ὅτι
Treg NIV RP

Here the inclusion of ὅτι (supported by Treg NIV RP) alters the syntax of the sentence and so requires a change in punctuation, from the full stop of WH to a comma. The textual note, therefore, indicates both the textual variants and the punctuation that corresponds with them.

The other is the use of ellipsis (…) in the textual notes. Sometimes it is used to save space, especially in variants involving word order. In Matt 15:37 (καὶ ἔφαγον πάντες καὶ ἐχορτάσθησαν, καὶ ⸂τὸ περισσεῦον τῶν κλασμάτων ἦραν⸃ ἑπτὰ σπυρίδας πλήρεις), for example, giving the full text of each variant would result in a textual note like this:

37 τὸ περισσεῦον τῶν κλασμάτων ἦραν WH
Treg NIV] ἦραν τὸ περισσεῦον τῶν κλασμάτων
RP

The use of ellipses to replace exactly the same words in each variant results in a shorter note:

37 τὸ ... κλασμάτων ἦραν WH Treg NIV] ἦραν
τὸ ... κλασμάτων RP.

In other cases the use of ellipses helps to make clear the places where two or more textual variants actually differ. In Acts 9:31, for example, the entire verse is enclosed by a pair of multiword variant markers (31 ⸀μὲν οὖν ἐκκλησία καθ᾽ ὅλης τῆς Ἰουδαίας καὶ Γαλιλαίας καὶ Σαμαρείας εἶχεν εἰρήνην οἰκοδομουμένη, καὶ πορευομένη τῷ φόβῳ τοῦ κυρίου καὶ τῇ παρακλήσει τοῦ ἁγίου πνεύματος ἐπληθύνετο⸃). The apparatus, however, looks like this:

**31 Ἡ ... ἐκκλησία ... εἶχεν ...
οἰκοδομουμένη ... πορευομένη ...
ἐπληθύνετο** WH Treg NIV] Αἱ ... ἐκκλησίαι
... εἶχον ... οἰκοδομούμεναι ... πορευόμεναι ...
ἐπληθύνοντο RP

Here the ellipses not only save space but also reveal clearly the places where the variant readings differ and the nature of the variation (singular versus plural).

I John

ΙΩΑΝΝΟΥ Α

I JOHN 1

New Vocabulary by Frequency [Chapter, Book, SBLGNT Occurrences]

κοινωνία, ας, ἡ, *close association, participation* [4, 4, 19]

ἀπαγγέλλω, *I report, proclaim, narrate* [2, 2, 45]

καθαρίζω, *I cleanse, purify, purge* [2, 2, 31]

φανερόω, *I make manifest, make known* [2, 9, 48]

ἀγγελία, ας, ἡ, *message, news, report* [1, 2, 2]

ἀδικία, ας, ἡ, *wrongdoing, injustice* [1, 2, 25]

ἁμαρτάνω, *I sin, miss the mark* [1, 10, 43]

ἀναγγέλλω, *I recount, report, teach* [1, 1, 14]

ἡμέτερος, α, ον, *our* (ref. to author) [1, 2, 7]

θεάομαι, *I observe, behold* [1, 3, 23]

ὁμολογέω, *I confess, admit* (in public) [1, 5, 26]

πλανάω, *I lead astray, deceive* [1, 3, 39]

σκοτία, ας, ἡ, *darkness, gloom* [1, 6, 17]

σκότος, ους, τό, *darkness, moral darkness* [1, 1, 30]

ψεύδομαι, *I lie, intentionally deceive* [1, 1, 12]

ψεύστης, ου, ὁ, *liar, cheat, fabricator* [1, 5, 10]

ψηλαφάω, *I handle, touch* [1, 1, 4]

ΙΩΑΝΝΟΥ Α

1.1 ῝Ο[1] ἦν ἀπ᾽ ἀρχῆς, ὃ ἀκηκόαμεν,[2] ὃ ἑωράκαμεν[3] τοῖς ὀφθαλμοῖς[4] ἡμῶν, ὃ ἐθεασάμεθα[5] καὶ αἱ χεῖρες ἡμῶν ἐψηλάφησαν,[6] περὶ τοῦ λόγου τῆς ζωῆς— ²καὶ ἡ ζωὴ ἐφανερώθη,[7] καὶ ἑωράκαμεν καὶ μαρτυροῦμεν καὶ ἀπαγγέλλομεν[8] ὑμῖν τὴν ζωὴν τὴν αἰώνιον ἥτις[9] ἦν πρὸς τὸν πατέρα καὶ ἐφανερώθη[7] ἡμῖν— ³ὃ ἑωράκαμεν καὶ ἀκηκόαμεν ἀπαγγέλλομεν[8] ⸀καὶ ὑμῖν, ἵνα καὶ ὑμεῖς κοινωνίαν[10] ἔχητε[11] μεθ᾽ ἡμῶν· καὶ[12]

---

1 TH: ὅ is a forward-pointing rel. prn.; occurs 5 times in 1Jn 1; *what, that which.*

2 MH: pf. stem of ἀκούω = ακου (root) › ακακου (redupl. of ακ + root) › ακηκου (lengthens init. root vowel) › ακηκο (reduc. of diph.) › ἀκηκοα (α is the pf. tense formative); occurs 3 times in 1Jn 1.

3 MH: pf. stem of ὁράω = ἑωρακα (κα is the pf. tense formative); occurs 3 times in 1Jn 1.

4 TH: dat. of means; *with our eyes.*

5 θεάομαι, *I observe, behold.*

6 ψηλαφάω, *I handle, touch.* MH: aor. stem of ψηλαφάω has a lengthened vowel (α › η) before tense formative, thus ἐψηλάφασαν › ἐψηλάφησαν.

7 φανερόω, *I make manifest, make known.*

8 ἀπαγγέλλω, *I report, proclaim, narrate.*

9 TH: indef. rel. pron. refers back to τὴν ζωήν and is the subject of ἦν.

10 κοινωνία, ας, ἡ, *close association, participation.*

11 MH: subj. mood has a lengthened connecting vowel (ε › η; ο › ω) and occurs 10 times in 1Jn 1.

12 TH: καί is additive and introduces κοινωνία as the topic; *moreover, also.*

ἡ κοινωνία¹ δὲ² ἡ ἡμετέρα³ μετὰ τοῦ πατρὸς καὶ μετὰ τοῦ υἱοῦ αὐτοῦ Ἰησοῦ Χριστοῦ· ⁴καὶ ταῦτα γράφομεν ⌜ἡμεῖς ἵνα ἡ χαρὰ ἡμῶν ᾖ πεπληρωμένη.⁴

⁵Καὶ ἔστιν αὕτη⁵ ἡ ἀγγελία⁶ ἣν ἀκηκόαμεν ἀπ' αὐτοῦ καὶ ἀναγγέλλομεν⁷ ὑμῖν, ὅτι⁸ ὁ θεὸς φῶς⁹ ἐστιν καὶ σκοτία¹⁰ ⌜ἐν αὐτῷ οὐκ ἔστιν⌝ οὐδεμία. ⁶ἐὰν¹¹ εἴπωμεν ὅτι κοινωνίαν¹ ἔχομεν μετ' αὐτοῦ καὶ ἐν τῷ σκότει¹² περιπατῶμεν, ψευδόμεθα¹³ καὶ οὐ ποιοῦμεν¹⁴ τὴν ἀλήθειαν· ⁷ἐὰν¹¹ δὲ¹⁵ ἐν τῷ φωτὶ περιπατῶμεν ὡς αὐτός ἐστιν ἐν τῷ φωτί, κοινωνίαν¹ ἔχομεν μετ' ἀλλήλων καὶ τὸ αἷμα ⌜Ἰησοῦ τοῦ υἱοῦ αὐτοῦ καθαρίζει¹⁶ ἡμᾶς ἀπὸ πάσης ἁμαρτίας. ⁸ἐὰν¹¹ εἴπωμεν ὅτι ἁμαρτίαν οὐκ ἔχομεν, ἑαυτοὺς πλανῶμεν¹⁷ καὶ ἡ ἀλήθεια ⌜οὐκ ἔστιν ἐν ἡμῖν⌝.

---

1 κοινωνία, ας, ἡ, close association, participation.
2 TH: δέ develops a new argument within the topic; additionally.
3 ἡμέτερος, α, ον, our (ref. to author).
4 TH: ᾖ πεπληρωμένη is a periphr. constr. (pres. εἰμί + pf. prtc. = pf. tense) parsed pf. mid./pass. subj. 3ʳᵈ sg.
5 TH: αὕτη is the pred. nom./adj. to the subject ἡ ἀγγελία.
6 ἀγγελία, ας, ἡ, message, news, report.
7 ἀναγγέλλω, I recount, report, teach.
8 TH: ὅτι marks indir. discourse; used 4 times in 1Jn 1.
9 TH: φῶς is the pred. nom. to the subject ὁ θεός.
10 σκοτία, ας, ἡ, darkness, gloom.
11 TH: protasis of a pres. general condition.
12 σκότος, ους, τό, darkness, moral darkness.
13 ψεύδομαι, I lie, intentionally deceive.
14 MH: the root (ποιε) ends in a vowel, so a connecting vowel will always contract (ε + ο = ου).
15 NA²⁸ does not retain δέ.
16 καθαρίζω, I cleanse, purify, purge.
17 πλανάω, I lead astray, deceive.

⁹ ἐὰν¹ ὁμολογῶμεν² τὰς ἁμαρτίας ἡμῶν, πιστός³ ἐστιν καὶ δίκαιος⁴ ἵνα ἀφῇ⁵ ἡμῖν τὰς ἁμαρτίας καὶ καθαρίσῃ⁶ ἡμᾶς ἀπὸ πάσης ἀδικίας.⁷ ¹⁰ ἐὰν¹ εἴπωμεν ὅτι οὐχ ἡμαρτήκαμεν,⁸ ψεύστην⁹ ποιοῦμεν¹⁰ αὐτὸν καὶ ὁ λόγος αὐτοῦ οὐκ ἔστιν ἐν ἡμῖν.

---

1   TH: protasis of a pres. general condition.

2   ὁμολογέω, *I confess, admit* (in public).

3   TH: πιστός is fronted for emphasis and is a pred. nom. to the subject "he" imbedded in the verb ἐστίν (pres. indic. 3ʳᵈ sg.).

4   TH: δίκαιος is a pred. nom. further defining the subject of ἐστίν.

5   MH: aor. act. subj. 3ʳᵈ sg. of ἀφίημι = ἀφη (aor. stem) + η (tense formative) + ι (3ʳᵈ sg. ending) › ἀφη + η (ι subscripts) › ἀφῇ (circumflex signals contraction of η + η).

6   καθαρίζω, *I cleanse, purify, purge.*

7   ἀδικία, ας, ἡ, *wrongdoing, injustice.*

8   ἁμαρτάνω, *I sin, miss the mark.* MH: pf. stem of ἁμαρτάνω = ἁμαρτ (root) › ἡμαρτ (redupl. causes α to lengthens to η) › ἡμαρτη (η is inserted; known as anaptyxis).

9   ψεύστης, ου, ὁ, *liar, cheat, fabricator.* TH: ψεύστην is the obj. complement in a double acc. constr., with αὐτόν as the obj.; ψεύστην is fronted for emphasis.

10   TH: ποιέω here has a double acc. constr.: subject makes obj. to be obj. complement.

I JOHN 2

New Vocabulary by Frequency [Chapter, Book, SBLGNT Occurrences]

σκοτία, ας, ἡ, *darkness, gloom* [5, 6, 16]

ἀντίχριστος, ου, ὁ, *False Messiah, One opposing the Messiah* [3, 4, 5]

ἀρνέομαι, *I deny, disown, disregard* [3, 3, 33]

ἐπιθυμία, ας, ἡ, *desire, long for, yearning* [3, 3, 38]

τεκνίον, ου, τό, *child, dear friend* [3, 7, 8]

χρῖσμα, ατος, τό, *anointment* [3, 3, 3]

ἀληθής, ές, *true, honest, real* [2, 2, 26]

ἁμαρτάνω, *I sin, miss the mark* [2, 10, 43]

καινός, ή, όν, *new, fresh, novel* [2, 2, 42]

μισέω, *I hate, hold in disfavor* [2, 5, 40]

νεανίσκος, ου, ὁ, *youth, young man, servant* [2, 2, 11]

νικάω, *I win, conquer, overcome* [2, 6, 28]

παλαιός, ά, όν, *old, ancient, aged* [2, 2, 19]

παράγω, *I intoduce, misled;* (Pass.) *passes away* [2, 2, 10]

φανερόω, *I make manifest, make known* [2, 9, 48]

ψεῦδος, ατος, τό, *lie, fabrication* [2, 2, 10]

ψεύστης, ου, ὁ, *liar, cheat, fabricator* [2, 5, 10]

αἰσχύνω, *I am ashamed, disgraced* [1, 1, 5]

ἀλαζονεία, ας, ἡ, *arrogance, false pretension* [1, 1, 2]

ἀληθινός, ή, όν, *true, trustworthy, authentic* [1, 4, 28]

ἀληθῶς, *truly, without a doubt* [1, 1, 18]

ἄρτι, *just now, presently* [1, 1, 36]

βίος, ου, ὁ, *life, livelihood, possession* [1, 2, 10]

ἐπαγγέλλομαι, *I promise, announce* (in public) [1, 1, 15]

ἡμέτερος, α, ον, *our* (ref. to author) [1, 2, 7]

ἱλασμός, οῦ, ὁ, *expiation, means of atonement* [1, 2, 2]

ἰσχυρός, ά, όν, *strong, mighty, powerful* [1, 1, 29]

ὅθεν, *therefore, whence, from where* [1, 1, 15]

ὁμολογέω, *I confess, admit* (in public) [1, 5, 26]

ὀφείλω, *I owe, am obligated;* (+inf) *I ought* [1, 3, 35]

παράκλητος, ου, ὁ, *encourager, legal assistant* [1, 1, 5]

παρουσία, ας, ἡ, *presence, arrival* [1, 1, 24]

παρρησία, ας, ἡ, *boldness, confidence, outspokenness* [1, 4, 31] πλανάω, *I lead astray, deceive* [1, 3, 39]

πού, *where, somewhere, anywhere* [1, 1, 7]

σκάνδαλον, ου, τό, *trap, stumbling-block* [1, 1, 15]

τελειόω, *I complete, perfect* [1, 4, 23]

τυφλόω, *I blind, make blind* [1, 1, 3]

φαίνω, *I shine, make appear* [1, 1, 31]

χρεία, ας, ἡ, *need, necessary thing* [1, 2, 49]

2.1 Τεκνία¹ μου, ταῦτα γράφω ὑμῖν ἵνα μὴ ἁμάρτητε.² καὶ ἐάν³ τις ἁμάρτῃ,⁴ παράκλητον⁵ ἔχομεν πρὸς τὸν πατέρα Ἰησοῦν⁶ Χριστὸν δίκαιον⁷, ²καὶ αὐτὸς ἱλασμός⁸ ἐστιν περὶ τῶν ἁμαρτιῶν ἡμῶν, οὐ περὶ τῶν ἡμετέρων⁹ δὲ¹⁰ μόνον¹¹ ἀλλὰ καὶ¹² περὶ ὅλου τοῦ κόσμου. ³Καὶ ἐν τούτῳ γινώσκομεν ὅτι ἐγνώκαμεν¹³ αὐτόν, ἐάν³ τὰς ἐντολὰς αὐτοῦ τηρῶμεν. ⁴ὁ λέγων ⌜ὅτι¹⁴ Ἔγνωκα αὐτὸν καὶ τὰς ἐντολὰς αὐτοῦ μὴ τηρῶν ψεύστης¹⁵ ἐστίν, καὶ ἐν τούτῳ ἡ ἀλήθεια οὐκ ἔστιν· ⁵ὃς δ' ἂν¹⁶ τηρῇ αὐτοῦ τὸν

---

1   τεκνίον, ου, τό, *child, dear friend*. TH: voc. case; occurs 10 times in 1Jn 2.
2   ἁμαρτάνω, *I sin, miss the mark*. MH: subj. mood has a lengthened connecting vowel (ε › η; ο › ω) and occurs 12 times in 1Jn 2. TH: with ἵνα indicates purpose.
3   TH: protasis of a pres. general condition.
4   ἁμαρτάνω, *I sin, miss the mark*.
5   παράκλητος, ου, ὁ, *encourager, legal assistant*.
6   TH: app. to παράκλητον.
7   TH: app. to either Χριστόν or παράκλητον.
8   ἱλασμός, οῦ, ὁ, *expiation, means of atonement*. TH: fronted pred. nom.
9   ἡμέτερος, α, ον, *our* (ref. to author).
10 TH: δέ develops a new argument within the topic; *additionally*.
11 TH: μόνον is a neut. adj. functioning adv. to modify the prep. phase; *additionally not only concerning our sins*.
12 TH: καί is additive; *also*.
13 MH: pf. stem of γινώσκω = γνο (root) › ἐγνο (init. consonant groups redupl. by adding ε) › ἐγνω (final vowel lengthens) › ἔγνωκα (pf. tense formative added); occurs 5 times in 1Jn 2.
14 TH: ὅτι introduces dir. discourse and is not translated; notice the capitalized Ἔγνωκα to indicate this.
15 ψεύστης, ου, ὁ, *liar, cheat, fabricator*.
16 TH: ὃς + ἄν = *whoever*; here forming a rel.-conditional clause, a pres. general condition.

λόγον, ἀληθῶς¹ ἐν τούτῳ ἡ ἀγάπη τοῦ θεοῦ τετελείωται.² ἐν τούτῳ γινώσκομεν ὅτι ἐν αὐτῷ ἐσμεν· ⁶ ὁ λέγων ἐν αὐτῷ μένειν³ ὀφείλει⁴ καθὼς ἐκεῖνος περιεπάτησεν καὶ ⌜αὐτὸς⁵ περιπατεῖν.⁶

⁷ ⌜Ἀγαπητοί, οὐκ ἐντολὴν καινὴν⁷ γράφω ὑμῖν, ἀλλ᾽ ἐντολὴν παλαιὰν⁸ ἣν εἴχετε⁹ ἀπ᾽ ἀρχῆς· ἡ ἐντολὴ ἡ παλαιά⁸ ἐστιν ὁ λόγος¹⁰ ὃν ⌜ἠκούσατε. ⁸ πάλιν¹¹ ἐντολὴν καινὴν⁷ γράφω ὑμῖν, ὅ ἐστιν ἀληθὲς¹² ἐν αὐτῷ καὶ ἐν ὑμῖν, ὅτι ἡ σκοτία¹³ παράγεται¹⁴ καὶ τὸ φῶς τὸ ἀληθινὸν¹⁵ ἤδη φαίνει.¹⁶ ⁹ ὁ λέγων ἐν τῷ φωτὶ εἶναι¹⁷ καὶ τὸν

1　ἀληθῶς, *truly, without a doubt.*
2　τελειόω, *I complete, perfect.* MH: pf. mid./pass. indic. 3ʳᵈ sg. of τελειόω = τελει (root) › τ (redupl.) + ε + τελειο › τετελειο + ται (3ʳᵈ sg. ending) › τετελείωται (final stem vowel lengthens; ο › ω).
3　TH: ὁ λέγων ἐν αὐτῷ μένειν, inf. as main verb of indir. discourse, *The one claiming that he remains in him.*
4　ὀφείλω, *I owe, am obligated;* (+inf) *I ought.*
5　TH: αὐτὸς is resuming the subject of ὀφείλει after the interruption of the adv. clause. NA has αὐτὸς [οὕτως] περιπατεῖν.
6　TH: complement to ὀφείλει.
7　καινός, ή, όν, *new, fresh, novel.*
8　παλαιός, ά, όν, *old, ancient, aged.*
9　MH: impf. act. indic. 2ⁿᵈ pl. of ἔχω = ε + ἐχ (pres. stem) › εἶχ (vowels contract; ε + ε = ει) › εἶχ + ε (thematic vowel) + τε (2ⁿᵈ pl. ending) › εἴχετε.
10　TH: pred. nom. to ἡ ἐντολή.
11　TH: *alternatively, on the other hand.*
12　ἀληθής, ές, *true, honest, real.*
13　σκοτία, ας, ἡ, *darkness, gloom.*
14　παράγω, *I introduce, mislead;* (Pass.) *passes away.*
15　ἀληθινός, ή, όν, *true, trustworthy, authentic.*
16　φαίνω, *I shine, make appear.*
17　TH: ὁ λέγων ἐν τῷ φωτὶ εἶναι, inf. as main verb of indir. discourse, *The one claiming that he is in the light.*

ἀδελφὸν αὐτοῦ μισῶν¹ ἐν τῇ σκοτίᾳ² ἐστὶν ἕως ἄρτι.³ ¹⁰ ὁ ἀγαπῶν τὸν ἀδελφὸν αὐτοῦ ἐν τῷ φωτὶ μένει, καὶ σκάνδαλον⁴ ἐν αὐτῷ οὐκ ἔστιν· ¹¹ ὁ δὲ μισῶν¹ τὸν ἀδελφὸν αὐτοῦ ἐν τῇ σκοτίᾳ² ἐστὶν καὶ ἐν τῇ σκοτίᾳ² περιπατεῖ, καὶ οὐκ οἶδεν ποῦ⁵ ὑπάγει, ὅτι ἡ σκοτία² ἐτύφλωσεν⁶ τοὺς ὀφθαλμοὺς αὐτοῦ.

¹² Γράφω ὑμῖν, τεκνία,⁷ ὅτι ἀφέωνται⁸ ὑμῖν αἱ ἁμαρτίαι διὰ τὸ ὄνομα αὐτοῦ· ¹³ γράφω ὑμῖν, πατέρες, ὅτι ἐγνώκατε τὸν⁹ ἀπ᾽ ἀρχῆς· γράφω ὑμῖν, νεανίσκοι,¹⁰ ὅτι νενικήκατε¹¹ τὸν πονηρόν.¹²

¹⁴ ⸂ἔγραψα ὑμῖν, παιδία, ὅτι ἐγνώκατε τὸν πατέρα· ἔγραψα ὑμῖν, πατέρες, ὅτι ἐγνώκατε τὸν ἀπ᾽ ἀρχῆς· ἔγραψα ὑμῖν, νεανίσκοι,¹⁰ ὅτι

---

1 μισέω, *I hate, hold in disfavor.*
2 σκοτία, ας, ἡ, *darkness, gloom.*
3 ἄρτι, *just now, presently.* ΤΗ: ἕως ἄρτι, *currently.*
4 σκάνδαλον, ου, τό, *trap, stumbling-block.*
5 πού, *where, somewhere, anywhere.*
6 τυφλόω, *I blind, make blind.*
7 τεκνίον, ου, τό, *child, dear friend.*
8 ΜΗ: pf. mid./pass. indic. 3ʳᵈ pl. of ἀφίημι = ἀφει (pf. mid./pass.
   stem) + ο (thematic vowel) + νται (3ʳᵈ pl. ending) › ἀφειονται
   › ἀφέωνται (transfer of vowel quality; ει + ο › ε + ω).
9 ΤΗ: τόν is a substantiver making ἀπ᾽ ἀρχῆς the dir. obj. of
   ἐγνώκατε; also the masc. art. refers to a pers. rather than a
   concept; *the one who is from the beginning.*
10 νεανίσκος, ου, ὁ, *youth, young man, servant.*
11 νικάω, *I win, conquer, overcome.* ΜΗ: pf. stem of νικάω = νικα
   (root) › νενικα (redupl. ν + ε) › νενικη (lengthens final vowel;
   α › η) › νενικηκ (pf. tense formative added); occurs twice in
   1Jn 2.
12 ΤΗ: this subst. adj. refers to a person because of the masc. art.;
   the Evil One.

ἰσχυροί¹ ἐστε καὶ ὁ λόγος τοῦ θεοῦ ἐν ὑμῖν μένει καὶ νενικήκατε² τὸν πονηρόν. ¹⁵ Μὴ ἀγαπᾶτε³ τὸν κόσμον μηδὲ τὰ⁴ ἐν τῷ κόσμῳ. ἐάν⁵ τις ἀγαπᾷ⁶ τὸν κόσμον, οὐκ ἔστιν ἡ ἀγάπη τοῦ πατρὸς ἐν αὐτῷ· ¹⁶ ὅτι πᾶν⁷ τὸ⁸ ἐν τῷ κόσμῳ, ἡ ἐπιθυμία⁹ τῆς σαρκὸς καὶ ἡ ἐπιθυμία⁹ τῶν ὀφθαλμῶν καὶ ἡ ἀλαζονεία¹⁰ τοῦ βίου,¹¹ οὐκ ἔστιν ἐκ τοῦ πατρός, ἀλλὰ ἐκ τοῦ κόσμου ἐστίν· ¹⁷ καὶ ὁ κόσμος παράγεται¹² καὶ ἡ ἐπιθυμία¹³ αὐτοῦ, ὁ δὲ ποιῶν τὸ θέλημα τοῦ θεοῦ μένει εἰς τὸν αἰῶνα.¹⁴

¹⁸ Παιδία, ἐσχάτη ὥρα¹⁵ ἐστίν,¹⁶ καὶ καθὼς

---

1 ἰσχυρός, ά, όν, *strong, mighty, powerful.* TH: fronted pred. nom.

2 νικάω, *I win, conquer, overcome.*

3 MH: final vowel of the root (ἀγαπα) contracts with the thematic vowel (α + ε = ᾶ).

4 TH: τά is a substantiver and refers to a concept; *the things in the world.*

5 TH: protasis of a pres. general condition.

6 MH: final vowel of the root (ἀγαπα) contracts with the thematic vowel (α + ε = ᾶ) and then the iota subscripts (ᾶ + ι = ᾷ).

7 TH: πᾶς is functioning attrib.

8 TH: τό is a substantiver and is being attrib. modified by πᾶν; *everything.*

9 ἐπιθυμία, ας, ἡ, *desire, long for, yearning.* TH: app. to πᾶν τὸ ἐν τῷ κόσμῳ.

10 ἀλαζονεία, ας, ἡ, *arrogance, false pretension;* **pride**. TH: app. to πᾶν τὸ ἐν τῷ κόσμῳ.

11 βίος, ου, ὁ, *life, livelihood, possession.* TH: ἡ ἀλαζονεία τοῦ βίου, (idiomatic) *the arrogance in one's lifestyle.*

12 παράγω, *I introduce, mislead;* (Pass.) *passes away.*

13 ἐπιθυμία, ας, ἡ, *desire, long for, yearning.*

14 TH: εἰς τὸν αἰῶνα; *everlastingly, forevermore.*

15 TH: ἐσχάτη ὥρα is the pred. nom. to subj. of ἐστίν.

16 TH: (lit.) *it is the last hour;* (idiomatic) *this is the last chance.*

ἠκούσατε ⌜ὅτι¹ ἀντίχριστος² ἔρχεται, καὶ
νῦν ἀντίχριστοι² πολλοὶ γεγόνασιν³· ὅθεν⁴
γινώσκομεν ὅτι ἐσχάτη ὥρα ἐστίν.⁵ ¹⁹ ἐξ ἡμῶν
ἐξῆλθαν,⁶ ἀλλ᾽ οὐκ ἦσαν ἐξ ἡμῶν· εἰ⁷ γὰρ ⌜ἐξ
ἡμῶν ἦσαν⌝, μεμενήκεισαν⁸ ἂν⁹ μεθ᾽ ἡμῶν·
ἀλλ᾽ ἵνα φανερωθῶσιν¹⁰ ὅτι οὐκ εἰσὶν πάντες
ἐξ ἡμῶν. ²⁰ καὶ¹¹ ὑμεῖς χρῖσμα¹² ἔχετε ἀπὸ τοῦ
ἁγίου ⌜καὶ οἴδατε¹³ ⌜πάντες·¹⁴ ²¹ οὐκ ἔγραψα ὑμῖν

---

1 TH: ὅτι marks indir. discourse.
2 ἀντίχριστος, ου, ὁ, *False Messiah, One opposing the Messiah;*
   Messiah Opposition.
3 MH: pf. stem of γίνομαι = γεν (root) › γεγεν (redupl. γ + ε) ›
   γεγον (ε undergoes a qualitative vowel gradation to an ο).
4 ὅθεν, *therefore, whence, from where.*
5 TH: (lit.) *it is the last hour;* (idiomatic) *this is the last chance.*
6 MH: suppl. aor. indic. stem of ἐξέρχομαι = ἐκ + ἐλευθ (suppl.
   root) › ἐξ (εκσ is the root, σ is retained before a vowel; κ + ς
   = ξ, known as affrication) + ἐλθευ (ευ and θ change places;
   known as metathesis) › ἐξ + ἠλθευ (hist. aug. causes ε to
   lengthens to η) › ἐξῆλ (ευ drops out; known as apocope).
7 TH: protasis of a past contrary-to-fact condition.
8 MH: plpf. act. indic. 3ʳᵈ pl. from μένω = μεν (root) › μεμεν
   (redupl. μ + ε) › μεμενη (η is inserted; known as anaptyxis) ›
   μεμενη (pf. stem) + κ (tense formative) + ει (thematic vowel;
   Mounce §45.6) + σαν (3ʳᵈ pl. ending) › μεμενηκεισαν; *they*
   had remained.
9 TH: apodosis of the past contrary-to-fact condition; the presence
   of ἂν helps identify this construction and marks possibility;
   would.
10 φανερόω, *I make manifest, make known.* MH: aor. pass. subj. 3ʳᵈ
   pl. of φανερόω = φανερο (root) + θ (tense formative) + ωσιν
   (3ʳᵈ pl ending with moveable nu; lengthened connecting vowel
   is the subj. mood formative; ο › ω) › φανερωθωσιν (final root
   vowel lengthens in subj. mood; ο › ω).
11 TH: additive καί; *moreover.*
12 χρῖσμα, ατος, τό, *anointment.*
13 TH: verse 21 is possibly the obj. or content of οἴδατε.
14 TH: this nom. adj. is functioning attrib. to further focus on the
   subject of οἴδατε; *everyone of you knows.*

ὅτι οὐκ οἴδατε τὴν ἀλήθειαν, ἀλλ' ὅτι οἴδατε
αὐτήν, καὶ¹ ὅτι πᾶν² ψεῦδος³ ἐκ τῆς ἀληθείας
οὐκ ἔστιν. ²² τίς ἐστιν ὁ ψεύστης⁴ εἰ μὴ ὁ
ἀρνούμενος⁵ ὅτι⁶ Ἰησοῦς οὐκ ἔστιν ὁ χριστός;
οὗτός ἐστιν ὁ ἀντίχριστος,⁷ ὁ ἀρνούμενος⁸ τὸν
πατέρα καὶ τὸν υἱόν. ²³ πᾶς ὁ ἀρνούμενος⁵ τὸν
υἱὸν οὐδὲ⁹ τὸν πατέρα ἔχει· ⸀ὁ ὁμολογῶν¹⁰ τὸν
υἱὸν καὶ¹¹ τὸν πατέρα ἔχει⸃. ²⁴ ⸀ὑμεῖς¹² ὃ ἠκούσατε
ἀπ' ἀρχῆς, ἐν ὑμῖν μενέτω·¹³ ἐὰν¹⁴ ἐν ὑμῖν μείνῃ
ὃ¹⁵ ἀπ' ἀρχῆς ἠκούσατε, καὶ ὑμεῖς ἐν τῷ υἱῷ
καὶ ἐν τῷ πατρὶ μενεῖτε.¹⁶ ²⁵ καὶ αὕτη ἐστὶν ἡ
ἐπαγγελία ἣν αὐτὸς ἐπηγγείλατο¹⁷ ἡμῖν, τὴν

---

1 TH: additive καί; *moreover, additionally.*
2 TH: attrib. adj. modifying ψεῦδος; *any lie.*
3 ψεῦδος, ατος, τό, *lie, fabrication.*
4 ψεύστης, ου, ὁ, *liar, cheat, fabricator.* TH: pred. nom.
5 ἀρνέομαι, *I deny, disown, disregard.*
6 TH: ὅτι marks indir. discourse.
7 ἀντίχριστος, ου, ὁ, *False Messiah, One opposing the Messiah;*
   Messiah Opposition. TH: pred. nom.
8 ἀρνέομαι, *I deny, disown, disregard.* TH: appositional to ὁ
   ἀντιχριστος.
9 TH: *additionally neither.*
10 ὁμολογέω, *I confess, admit* (in public).
11 TH: additive καί; *moreover, also.*
12 TH: pendent nom. of reference (ὑμεῖς is the new topic); *As for*
    you all.
13 TH: the fronted rel. clause is the subject of μενέτω; *what you all*
    heard from the beginning must remain with you all.
14 TH: protasis of a pres. general condition.
15 TH: rel. clause is the subject of μείνῃ.
16 MH: fut. act. indic. 2ⁿᵈ pl. of μένω = μεν (root) + εσ (tense
    formative) + ετε (thematic 2ⁿᵈ pl. ending) › μενεετε (σ btw. 2
    vowels elides) › μενεῖτε (vowels contract; ε + ε = εῖ).
17 ἐπαγγέλλομαι, *I promise, announce* (in public).

ζωὴν¹ τὴν αἰώνιον.
²⁶ Ταῦτα ἔγραψα ὑμῖν περὶ τῶν πλανώντων²
ὑμᾶς. ²⁷ καὶ ὑμεῖς³ τὸ χρῖσμα⁴ ὃ ἐλάβετε⁵ ἀπ᾽
αὐτοῦ ⸀μένει ἐν ὑμῖν⸀, καὶ οὐ χρείαν⁶ ἔχετε ἵνα
τις⁷ διδάσκῃ ὑμᾶς· ἀλλ᾽ ὡς τὸ ⸀αὐτοῦ χρῖσμα⁸
διδάσκει ὑμᾶς περὶ πάντων, καὶ⁹ ἀληθές¹⁰ ἐστιν
καὶ οὐκ ἔστιν ψεῦδος,¹¹ καὶ καθὼς ἐδίδαξεν¹²
ὑμᾶς, ⸀μένετε¹³ ἐν αὐτῷ.

²⁸ Καὶ νῦν, τεκνία,¹⁴ μένετε¹³ ἐν αὐτῷ, ἵνα
⸀ἐὰν¹⁵ φανερωθῇ¹⁶ ⸀σχῶμεν¹⁷ παρρησίαν¹⁸ καὶ μὴ

---

1 TH: app. to ἤν, which refers to ἡ ἐπαγγελία.
2 πλανάω, I lead astray, deceive.
3 TH: pendent nom. of reference (ὑμεῖς is the topic; also the
   subject of the following rel. pron. clause, ὃ ἐλάβετε…) with
   an additive καί; Also, focusing on you all, the anointing that
   you all received…
4 χρῖσμα, ατος, τό, anointment. TH: subject of μένει.
5 TH: aor. indic. stem of λαμβάνω = λαβ (root) › ἐλαβ (hist. aug.
   added).
6 χρεία, ας, ἡ, need, necessary thing.
7 TH: indef. pron.
8 χρῖσμα, ατος, τό, anointment.
9 TH: καί…καί; both…and.
10 ἀληθής, ές, true, honest, real. TH: pred. nom.
11 ψεῦδος, ατος, τό, lie, fabrication. TH: pred. nom.
12 MH: aor. act. indic. 3rd sg. of δίδασκω = διδαχ (root; Smyth
   §447a) › ἐδιδαχ (hist. aug. added) › ἐδιδαχ + σα (tense
   formative) › ἐδιδαξα (χ + ς = ξ; known as affrication) ›
   ἐδίδαξεν (α › ε to distinguish from 1st sg. ending; ν is a
   moveable nu).
13 TH: can be indic. or impv.; context dictates μένετε is impv.
14 τεκνίον, ου, τό, child, dear friend.
15 TH: protasis of a pres. general condition.
16 φανερόω, I make manifest, make known.
17 TH: aor. stem of ἔχω = σεχ (root) › σχ (ε drops out; known as
   syncope).
18 παρρησία, ας, ἡ, boldness, confidence, outspokenness.

αἰσχυνθῶμεν¹ ἀπ' αὐτοῦ ἐν τῇ παρουσίᾳ² αὐτοῦ.
²⁹ ἐὰν³ εἰδῆτε⁴ ὅτι δίκαιός⁵ ἐστιν, γινώσκετε
⌜ὅτι⁶ πᾶς ὁ ποιῶν τὴν δικαιοσύνην ἐξ αὐτοῦ
γεγέννηται.⁷

---

1 αἰσχύνω, *I am ashamed, disgraced.*
2 παρουσία, ας, ἡ, *presence, arrival.*
3 TH: protasis of a pres. general condition.
4 MH: pf. act. subj. 2nd pl. of οἶδα = ϝιδ (root) › ϝεϝιδ (redupl.
   of ϝ + ε) › εϝιδ (init. ϝ drops out; known as aphaeresis) › ειδ
   (intervocalic ϝ drops out) › ειδ + ετε (2nd pl. ending) › εἰδῆτε
   (subj. lengthens connecting vowel; ε › η).
5 TH: pred. nom. subst. adj.
6 NA has ὅτι καὶ πᾶς.
7 MH: pf. stem of γεννάω = γεννα (root) › γεγεννα (redupl. γ +
   ε) › γεγεννη (final vowel lengthens).

I JOHN 3

New Vocabulary by Frequency [Chapter, Book, SBLGNT Occurrences]

ἁμαρτάνω, I sin, miss the mark [4, 10, 43]

διάβολος, ου, slanderous, hostile, devilish; (Subst.) Devil [4, 4, 37]

φανερόω, I make manifest, make known [4, 9, 48]

ἀνθρωποκτόνος, ου, ὁ, murderer [2, 2, 3]

ἀνομία, ας, ἡ, unlawfulness, lawlessness [2, 2, 15]

καταγινώσκω, I condemn, find guilty [2, 2, 3]

μισέω, I hate, hold in disfavor [2, 5, 40]

σφάζω, I murder, butcher, slaughter [2, 2, 10]

τεκνίον, ου, τό, child, dear friend [2, 7, 8]

ἀγγελία, ας, ἡ, message, news, report [1, 2, 2]

ἁγνίζω, I purify, cleanse (away) [1, 1, 7]

ἁγνός, ή, όν, pure, cleansed [1, 1, 8]

ἀρεστός, ή, όν, acceptable, satisfying [1, 1, 4]

βίος, ου, ὁ, life, livelihood, possession [1, 2, 10]

ἔμπροσθεν, (+gen) in front of, before [1, 1, 48]

θαυμάζω, I am impressed, amazed [1, 1, 43]

Κάϊν, ὁ, Cain [1, 1, 3]

κλείω, I block, shut, close [1, 1, 16]

λύω, I undo, release, destroy [1, 1, 42]

μεταβαίνω, I move, change, go [1, 1, 12]

ὅμοιος, οία, οιον, likewise, similar, like [1, 1, 45]

οὔπω, not yet, still not [1, 1, 26]

ὀφείλω, I owe, am obligated; (+inf) I ought [1, 3, 35]

παρρησία, ας, ἡ, boldness, confidence, outspokenness [1, 4, 31]

πλανάω, I lead astray, deceive [1, 3, 39]

ποταπός, ή, όν, what kind of, what sort of [1, 1, 7]

σπέρμα, ατος, τό, seed, descendent [1, 1, 43]

σπλάγχνον, ου, τό, innards; (metaph.) heart, feelings [1, 1, 11]

φανερός, ά, όν, visible, known, exposed [1, 1, 18]

χάριν, (+gen) for, on account of [1, 1, 9]

χρεία, ας, ἡ, need, necessary thing [1, 2, 49]

3.1 ἴδετε¹ ποταπὴν² ἀγάπην³ δέδωκεν⁴ ἡμῖν ὁ πατήρ⁵ ἵνα τέκνα θεοῦ κληθῶμεν,⁶ ⸀καὶ ἐσμέν⸀.⁷ διὰ τοῦτο ὁ κόσμος οὐ γινώσκει ⸀ἡμᾶς ὅτι οὐκ ἔγνω⁸ αὐτόν. ²ἀγαπητοί,⁹ νῦν τέκνα θεοῦ ἐσμεν, καὶ οὔπω¹⁰ ἐφανερώθη¹¹ τί ἐσόμεθα.¹² ⸀οἴδαμεν ὅτι ἐὰν¹³ φανερωθῇ¹⁴ ὅμοιοι¹⁵ αὐτῷ ἐσόμεθα, ὅτι ὀψόμεθα¹⁶ αὐτὸν καθώς ἐστιν. ³καὶ πᾶς ὁ ἔχων

---

1   MH: aor. suppl. of ὁράω = ϝιδ (root) › ιδ (init. ϝ drops out; known as aphaeresis).

2   ποταπός, ή, όν, *what kind of, what sort of.* TH: emphasizes quality.

3   TH: fronted dir. obj.

4   MH: pf. stem of δίδωμι = δο (root) › δεδο (redupl. δ + ε) › δεδω (final vowel lengthens) › δεδωκ (pf. tense formative added).

5   TH: subject of δέδωκεν.

6   MH: aor. pass. subj. 1ˢᵗ pl. of κάλεω = καλε (root) › κλαε (α and λ change places; known as metathesis) › κλα (α + ε = α) › κλη (α undergoes quantitative vowel gradation to η) › κλη (aor. stem) + θη (pass. tense formative) + ωμεν (1ˢᵗ pl. ending; subj. mood lengthens connecting vowel) › κληθῶμεν (η + ω = ῶ).

7   TH: the obj. of ἐσμέν is gapped (implied/elliptical) from the previous clause (τέκνα θεοῦ); *we are children of God.*

8   MH: aor. act. indic. 3ʳᵈ sg. of γινώσκω = γνο (root) › γνω (final vowel lengthens) › ἔγνω (hist. aug. added; 3ʳᵈ sg. does not have a per. ending.).

9   TH: voc. case; occurs 5 times in 1Jn 3.

10 οὔπω, *not yet, still not.*

11 φανερόω, *I make manifest, make known.* MH: final stem vowel lengthens before the pass. tense formative (ο › ω). TH: the obj. of ἐφανερώθη is τί ἐσόμεθα.

12 TH: inter. pron. (pred. nom.) + fut. of εἰμί; *what we will be.*

13 TH: protasis of a pres. general condition.

14 φανερόω, *I make manifest, make known.* MH: final stem vowel lengthens before the pass. tense formative (ο › ω).

15 ὅμοιος, οία, οιον, *likewise, similar, like.*

16 MH: fut. suppl. stem of ὁράω = οπ (suppl. root) › οπς (fut. tense formative) › οψ (π + ς = ψ; known as affrication).

τὴν ἐλπίδα ταύτην¹ ἐπ' αὐτῷ ἁγνίζει² ἑαυτὸν καθὼς ἐκεῖνος ἁγνός³ ἐστιν. ⁴ Πᾶς ὁ ποιῶν τὴν ἁμαρτίαν καὶ⁴ τὴν ἀνομίαν⁵ ποιεῖ, καὶ ἡ ἁμαρτία ἐστὶν ἡ ἀνομία.⁵ ⁵ καὶ οἴδατε ὅτι ἐκεῖνος ἐφανερώθη⁶ ἵνα τὰς ⌐ἁμαρτίας ἄρῃ,⁷ καὶ⁸ ἁμαρτία ἐν αὐτῷ οὐκ ἔστιν. ⁶ πᾶς ὁ ἐν⁹ αὐτῷ μένων οὐχ ἁμαρτάνει·¹⁰ πᾶς ὁ ἁμαρτάνων¹⁰ οὐχ ἑώρακεν¹¹ αὐτὸν οὐδὲ¹² ἔγνωκεν¹³ αὐτόν. ⁷τεκνία,¹⁴ μηδεὶς πλανάτω¹⁵ ὑμᾶς· ὁ ποιῶν τὴν δικαιοσύνην δίκαιός¹⁶ ἐστιν, καθὼς ἐκεῖνος

---

1 TH: attrib. adj. that is typically in the pred. position.
2 ἁγνίζω, *I purify, cleanse (away)*. TH: the subject of ἁγνίζει is the prtc. phrase πᾶς ὁ ἔχων τὴν ἐλπίδα ταύτην ἐπ' αὐτῷ.
3 ἁγνός, ή, όν, *pure, cleansed*.
4 TH: additive καί; *also*.
5 ἀνομία, ας, ἡ, *unlawfulness, lawlessness*.
6 φανερόω, *I make manifest, make known*.
7 MH: aor. act. subj. 3ʳᵈ sg. of αἴρω = αρ (root; also aor. stem) › ἀρ + η (3rd sg. ending; subj. lengthens connecting vowel) › ἄρῃ.
8 TH: could be an additive καί; *also*.
9 TH: prep. phrase in the internal attrib. slot (1ˢᵗ attrib. position); *everyone remaining with him*.
10 ἁμαρτάνω, *I sin, miss the mark*.
11 MH: pf. stem of ὁράω = ϝορα (root; Smyth §431) › ϝεϝορα (redupl. of ϝ + ε + root) › ἐϝορα (init. ϝ dissim. into a rough breathing mark; Mounce §32.7) › ἑωρα (ϝ elides causing ο to lengthens to ω) › ἑωρακ (κ = pf. tense formative).
12 TH: *additionally neither*.
13 MH: pf. stem of γινώσκω = γνο (root) › ἐγνο (init. consonant groups redupl. by adding ε) › ἐγνω (final vowel lengthens) › ἐγνωκα (pf. tense formative added; κα › κε in 3ʳᵈ sg.); occurs twice in 1Jn 3.
14 τεκνίον, ου, τό, *child, dear friend*. NA²⁸ has παιδία.
15 πλανάω, *I lead astray, deceive*. MH: pres. act. impv. 3ʳᵈ sg. TH: subject is μηδείς.
16 TH: pred. nom.

δίκαιός¹ ἐστιν· ⁸ ὁ ποιῶν τὴν ἁμαρτίαν ἐκ τοῦ διαβόλου² ἐστίν, ὅτι ἀπ' ἀρχῆς ὁ διάβολος² ἁμαρτάνει.³ εἰς τοῦτο ἐφανερώθη⁴ ὁ υἱὸς τοῦ θεοῦ ἵνα λύσῃ⁵ τὰ ἔργα τοῦ διαβόλου.² ⁹ πᾶς ὁ γεγεννημένος ἐκ τοῦ θεοῦ ἁμαρτίαν οὐ ποιεῖ, ὅτι σπέρμα⁶ αὐτοῦ ἐν αὐτῷ μένει, καὶ οὐ δύναται ἁμαρτάνειν,⁷ ὅτι ἐκ τοῦ θεοῦ γεγέννηται. ¹⁰ ἐν τούτῳ φανερά⁸ ἐστιν τὰ τέκνα⁹ τοῦ θεοῦ καὶ τὰ τέκνα τοῦ διαβόλου·² πᾶς ὁ μὴ ποιῶν δικαιοσύνην οὐκ ἔστιν ἐκ τοῦ θεοῦ, καὶ ὁ μὴ ἀγαπῶν τὸν ἀδελφὸν αὐτοῦ.¹⁰ ¹¹ "Οτι¹¹ αὕτη ἐστὶν ἡ ἀγγελία¹² ἣν ἠκούσατε ἀπ' ἀρχῆς, ἵνα¹³ ἀγαπῶμεν ἀλλήλους· ¹² οὐ καθὼς Κάϊν¹⁴ ἐκ τοῦ πονηροῦ ἦν καὶ ἔσφαξεν¹⁵

---

1 TH: pred. nom.
2 διάβολος, ου, *slanderous, hostile, devilish;* (subst.) *Devil.*
3 ἁμαρτάνω, *I sin, miss the mark.* TH: pres. tense + ἀπ' ἀρχῆς = focus on the pres. verbal action that started in the past (much like a pf. tense); *the devil has been sinning from the beginning;* (or) *the devil sins and has been doing so from the beginning.*
4 φανερόω, *I make manifest, make known.*
5 λύω, *I undo, release, destroy.*
6 σπέρμα, ατος, τό, *seed, descendent;* **character.**
7 ἁμαρτάνω, *I sin, miss the mark.* TH: inf. complement of δύναται.
8 φανερός, ά, όν, *visible, known, exposed.* TH: pred. adj.
9 TH: neut. pl. noun can be the subject of a sg. verb; dual contrasting subject with τὰ τέκνα τοῦ διαβόλου.
10 TH: οὐκ ἔστιν ἐκ τοῦ θεοῦ is gapped (implied/elliptical).
11 TH: *for.*
12 ἀγγελία, ας, ἡ, *message, news, report;* **command.**
13 TH: noun/content clause.
14 Κάϊν, ὁ, *Cain.*
15 σφάζω, *I murder, butcher, slaughter.*

τὸν ἀδελφὸν αὐτοῦ· καὶ χάριν¹ τίνος ἔσφαξεν²
αὐτόν; ὅτι τὰ ἔργα αὐτοῦ πονηρὰ³ ἦν, τὰ δὲ
τοῦ ἀδελφοῦ αὐτοῦ δίκαια.⁴ ¹³ ⌐μὴ⁵ θαυμάζετε,⁶
⌐ἀδελφοί, εἰ μισεῖ⁷ ὑμᾶς ὁ κόσμος. ¹⁴ ἡμεῖς
οἴδαμεν ὅτι μεταβεβήκαμεν⁸ ἐκ τοῦ θανάτου
εἰς τὴν ζωήν, ὅτι ἀγαπῶμεν τοὺς ἀδελφούς· ὁ
μὴ ⌐ἀγαπῶν⁹ μένει ἐν τῷ θανάτῳ. ¹⁵ πᾶς ὁ μισῶν⁷
τὸν ἀδελφὸν αὐτοῦ ἀνθρωποκτόνος¹⁰ ἐστίν,
καὶ οἴδατε ὅτι πᾶς ἀνθρωποκτόνος¹⁰ οὐκ ἔχει
ζωὴν αἰώνιον ἐν ⌐αὐτῷ μένουσαν.¹¹ ¹⁶ ἐν τούτῳ
ἐγνώκαμεν τὴν ἀγάπην, ὅτι ἐκεῖνος ὑπὲρ ἡμῶν
τὴν ψυχὴν αὐτοῦ ἔθηκεν·¹² καὶ ἡμεῖς ὀφείλομεν¹³
ὑπὲρ τῶν ἀδελφῶν τὰς ψυχὰς ⌐θεῖναι.¹⁴ ¹⁷ ὃς δ'

---

1   χάριν, (+gen) *for, on account of; for reason of.*
2   σφάζω, *I murder, butcher, slaughter.* MH: ζ + ς (aor. formative)
    = ξ (known as affrication).
3   TH: pred. adj.
4   TH: pred. adj. with ἦν gapped (implied/elliptical).
5   NA has [Καὶ] μή.
6   θαυμάζω, *I am impressed, amazed.*
7   μισέω, *I hate, disregard.*
8   μεταβαίνω, *I move, change, go.* MH: pf. stem of μεταβαίνω =
    μετα + βα (root) › μετα + βεβα (redupl. β + ε) › μεταβεβη
    (final vowel lengthens) › μεταβεβηκα (κα = pf. tense
    formative).
9   TH: τοὺς ἀδελφούς is gapped (implied/elliptical) as the obj. of
    the prtc.
10 ἀνθρωποκτόνος, ου, ὁ, *murderer.*
11 TH: the participle μένουσαν modifies ζωήν.
12 MH: aor. indic. stem of τίθημι = θε (root) › ἐθε (hist. aug.
    added) › ἐθη (final vowel lengthens) › ἐθηκ (κ = aor. tense
    formative); *he laid down, he gave up.*
13 ὀφείλω, *I owe, am obligated;* (+inf) *I ought.*
14 TH: θεῖναι is the complement of ὀφείλομεν; *to lay down, to
    give up.*

ἂν¹ ἔχῃ² τὸν βίον³ τοῦ κόσμου καὶ θεωρῇ τὸν
ἀδελφὸν αὐτοῦ χρείαν⁴ ἔχοντα⁵ καὶ κλείσῃ⁶ τὰ
σπλάγχνα⁷ αὐτοῦ ἀπ' αὐτοῦ, πῶς ἡ ἀγάπη τοῦ
θεοῦ μένει ἐν αὐτῷ;

18 ⸀Τεκνία,⁸ μὴ ἀγαπῶμεν⁹ λόγῳ¹⁰ μηδὲ τῇ¹⁰
γλώσσῃ ἀλλὰ¹¹ ἐν¹² ἔργῳ καὶ ἀληθείᾳ. **19** ⸀ἐν¹³
τούτῳ ⸀γνωσόμεθα ὅτι ἐκ τῆς ἀληθείας ἐσμέν,
καὶ ἔμπροσθεν¹⁴ αὐτοῦ πείσομεν¹⁵ ⸀τὴν καρδίαν⸀
ἡμῶν ²⁰ ὅτι¹⁶ ἐὰν¹⁷ καταγινώσκῃ¹⁸ ἡμῶν¹⁹ ἡ καρδία,

1　TH: ὃς δ' ἄν; indicates rel.-conditional clause, a pres. general
　　condition; *additionally whoever.*
2　MH: subj. of ἔχω with lengthened connecting vowel (ει > ηι > ῃ).
3　βίος, ου, ὁ, *life, livelihood, possession.*
4　χρεία, ας, ἡ, *need, necessary thing.* TH: obj. of ἔχοντα.
5　TH: the participle ἔχοντα modifies ἀδελφόν.
6　κλείω, *I block, shut, close.*
7　σπλάγχνον, ου, τό, *innards;* (metaph.) *heart, feelings.*
8　τεκνίον, ου, τό, *child, dear friend.*
9　TH: neg. hortatory subj.; *we must not love.*
10　TH: dat. of means; *by means of.*
11　NA²⁸ has ἀλλ'.
12　TH: modifies the gapped (implied/elliptical) ἀγαπῶμεν; *but we
　　must love by means of action and truthfulness.*
13　NA has [Καὶ] ἐν.
14　ἔμπροσθεν, (+gen) *in front of, before.*
15　MH: fut. stem of πείθω = πειθ (root) + ς (fut. tense formative) >
　　πεισσ (θ assimilates to σ) > πεισ (geminate σ partially reduce
　　to a single σ).
16　TH: marks indir. discourse.
17　TH: protasis of a pres. general condition.
18　καταγινώσκω, *I condemn, find guilty.*
19　TH: verbs of accusing take a gen. as the dir. obj.; *if the heart
　　should condemn us.*

ὅτι¹ μείζων² ἐστὶν³ ὁ θεὸς τῆς καρδίας⁴ ἡμῶν καὶ γινώσκει³ πάντα. ²¹ ἀγαπητοί, ἐὰν⁵ ἡ καρδία⁶ ⸀μὴ καταγινώσκῃ⁷ ἡμῶν⸀,⁸ παρρησίαν⁹ ἔχομεν πρὸς τὸν θεόν, ²² καὶ ὃ ⸀ἐὰν¹⁰ αἰτῶμεν λαμβάνομεν ⸀ἀπ᾽ αὐτοῦ, ὅτι τὰς ἐντολὰς αὐτοῦ τηροῦμεν¹¹ καὶ τὰ ἀρεστὰ¹² ἐνώπιον αὐτοῦ ποιοῦμεν. ²³ καὶ αὕτη ἐστὶν ἡ ἐντολὴ αὐτοῦ, ἵνα ⸀πιστεύσωμεν¹³ τῷ ὀνόματι τοῦ υἱοῦ αὐτοῦ Ἰησοῦ Χριστοῦ καὶ ἀγαπῶμεν ἀλλήλους, καθὼς ἔδωκεν¹⁴ ἐντολὴν ⸀ἡμῖν. ²⁴ καὶ ὁ τηρῶν τὰς ἐντολὰς αὐτοῦ ἐν αὐτῷ μένει καὶ αὐτὸς¹⁵ ἐν αὐτῷ· καὶ ἐν τούτῳ γινώσκομεν ὅτι μένει ἐν ἡμῖν, ἐκ τοῦ πνεύματος οὗ ἡμῖν ἔδωκεν.

1　TH: marks indir. discourse.
2　TH: comp. nom. sg. adj. form of μέγας functioning as a fronted pred. nom.; *greater than*.
3　TH: gnomic pres. stating a general truth.
4　TH: gen. of comparison; *God is greater than our heart*.
5　TH: protasis of a pres. general condition.
6　NA has ἡ καρδία [ἡμῶν] μὴ καταγινώσκῃ.
7　καταγινώσκω, *I condemn, find guilty*.
8　TH: verbs of accusing take a gen. as the dir. obj.; *if the heart does not condemn us*.
9　παρρησία, ας, ἡ, *boldness, confidence, outspokenness*.
10　TH: protasis of a pres. general condition; ὃ ἐάν, *whatever*.
11　MH: the root (τηρέω) ends in a vowel, so a connecting vowel will always contract (ε + ο = ου).
12　ἀρεστός, ή, όν, *acceptable, satisfying*. TH: subst. adj.; *the acceptable things*.
13　TH: πιστεύω can take a dat. as the dir. obj.; *we should believe in*.
14　MH: aor. indic. stem of δίδωμι = δο (root) › ἐδο (hist. aug.) › ἐδω (final vowel lengthens) › ἐδωκ (aor. tense formative added); occurs twice in 1Jn 3.
15　TH: subject of the gapped (implied/elliptical) verb μένει.

I JOHN 4

New Vocabulary by Frequency [Chapter, Book, SBLGNT Occurrences]

ὁμολογέω, *I confess, admit* (in public) [3, 5, 26]

τελειόω, *I complete, perfect* [3, 4, 23]

φόβος, ου, ὁ, *fear, intimidation, respect* [3, 3, 47]

θεάομαι, *I observe, behold* [2, 3, 23]

ἀντίχριστος, ου, ὁ, *False Messiah, One opposing the Messiah* [1, 4, 5]

δοκιμάζω, *I examine, investigate, demonstrate* [1, 1, 22]

ἱλασμός, οῦ, ὁ, *expiation, means of atonement* [1, 2, 2]

κόλασις, εως, ἡ, *punishment, correction* [1, 1, 2]

κρίσις, εως, ἡ, *judgment, punishment, justice* [1, 1, 47]

μισέω, *I hate, hold in disfavor* [1, 5, 40]

μονογενής, ές, *single, only, unique* [1, 1, 9]

νικάω, *I win, conquer, overcome* [1, 6, 28]

ὀφείλω, *I owe, am obligated;* (+inf) *I ought* [1, 3, 35]

παρρησία, ας, ἡ, *boldness, confidence, outspokenness* [1, 4, 31]

πλάνη, ης, ἡ, *deception, error, fraud* [1, 1, 10]

πώποτε, *yet, ever, at any point* [1, 1, 6]

σωτήρ, ῆρος, ὁ, *savior, champion, preserver* [1, 1, 24]

τεκνίον, ου, τό, *child, dear friend* [1, 7, 8]

τέλειος, α, ον, *complete, perfect, genuine* [1, 1, 19]

φανερόω, *I make manifest, make known* [1, 9, 48]

ψευδοπροφήτης, ου, ὁ, *false prophet, lying prophet* [1, 1, 11]

ψεύστης, ου, ὁ, *liar, cheat, fabricator* [1, 5, 10]

4.1 Ἀγαπητοί,¹ μὴ² παντὶ πνεύματι πιστεύετε, ἀλλὰ δοκιμάζετε³ τὰ πνεύματα εἰ ἐκ τοῦ θεοῦ ἐστιν,⁴ ὅτι πολλοὶ ψευδοπροφῆται⁵ ἐξεληλύθασιν⁶ εἰς τὸν κόσμον. ² ἐν τούτῳ ⌜γινώσκετε⁷ τὸ πνεῦμα τοῦ θεοῦ· πᾶν πνεῦμα⁸ ὃ ὁμολογεῖ⁹ Ἰησοῦν Χριστὸν ἐν σαρκὶ ἐληλυθότα¹⁰ ἐκ τοῦ θεοῦ ἐστιν, ³ καὶ πᾶν πνεῦμα¹¹ ὃ μὴ ὁμολογεῖ⁹ ⌜τὸν ⌜¹Ἰησοῦν ἐκ τοῦ θεοῦ οὐκ ἔστιν· καὶ τοῦτό ἐστιν τὸ¹² τοῦ ἀντιχρίστου,¹³ ὃ

---

1 TH: voc. case; occurs 4 times in 1Jn 4.
2 TH: marks the verb as non-indic. mood.
3 δοκιμάζω, I examine, investigate, demonstrate. TH: could be indic. or impv.; context suggests impv.
4 TH: τὰ πνεύματα is gapped (implied/elliptical) as the subject; neut. pl. noun can be the subject of a sg. verb; if they are from God.
5 ψευδοπροφήτης, ου, ὁ, false prophet, lying prophet.
6 MH: suppl. pf. stem of ἐξέρχομαι = ἐκ + ἐλευθ (suppl. root) › ἐξ (εκσ is the root, σ is retained before a vowel; κ + ς = ξ, known as affrication) + ἐλυθ (ευ undergoes a qualitative vowel gradation) › ἐξ + ἐλελυθ (redupl. ελ) › ἐξεληλυθ (lengthens init. root vowel).
7 TH: could be indic. or impv.; context suggests impv.
8 TH: subject of ἐστιν.
9 ὁμολογέω, I confess, admit (in public).
10 TH: obj. complement in a double acc. constr. with Ἰησοῦν as the obj. MH: suppl. pf. stem of ἔρχομαι = ἐλευθ (suppl. root) › ἐλυθ (ευ undergoes a qualitative vowel gradation) › ἐλελυθ (redupl. ελ) › ἐληλυθ (lengthens init. root vowel).
11 TH: subject of ἔστιν.
12 TH: substantiver probably in ref. to πνεῦμα; (lit.) the one of Messiah Opposition.
13 ἀντίχριστος, ου, ὁ, False Messiah, One opposing the Messiah; **Messiah Opposition.**

ἀκηκόατε¹ ὅτι² ἔρχεται, καὶ νῦν ἐν τῷ κόσμῳ
ἐστὶν ἤδη. ⁴ ὑμεῖς ἐκ τοῦ θεοῦ ἐστε, τεκνία,³
καὶ νενικήκατε⁴ αὐτούς, ὅτι μείζων⁵ ἐστὶν ὅ⁶ ἐν
ὑμῖν ἤ⁷ ὁ⁸ ἐν τῷ κόσμῳ· ⁵ αὐτοὶ ἐκ τοῦ κόσμου
εἰσίν· διὰ τοῦτο ἐκ τοῦ κόσμου λαλοῦσιν⁹ καὶ
ὁ κόσμος αὐτῶν¹⁰ ἀκούει.¹¹ ⁶ ἡμεῖς ἐκ τοῦ θεοῦ
ἐσμεν· ὁ¹² γινώσκων τὸν θεὸν ἀκούει¹¹ ἡμῶν,¹⁰
ὃς¹³ οὐκ ἔστιν ἐκ τοῦ θεοῦ οὐκ ἀκούει¹¹ ἡμῶν.¹⁰
ἐκ τούτου γινώσκομεν τὸ πνεῦμα τῆς ἀληθείας
καὶ¹⁴ τὸ πνεῦμα τῆς πλάνης.¹⁵

⁷ Ἀγαπητοί, ἀγαπῶμεν¹⁶ ἀλλήλους, ὅτι ἡ
ἀγάπη ἐκ τοῦ θεοῦ ἐστιν, καὶ πᾶς ὁ ἀγαπῶν

1　MH: pf. stem of ἀκούω = ακου (root) › ακακου (redupl. of ακ +
　　root) › ακηκου (lengthens init. root vowel) › ακηκο (reduc. of
　　diph.).
2　TH: marks indir. discourse.
3　τεκνίον, ου, τό, child, dear friend.
4　νικάω, I win, conquer, overcome. MH: pf. stem of νικάω = νικα
　　(root) › νενικα (redupl. ν + ε) › νενικη (lengthens final vowel;
　　α › η) › νενικηκ (pf. tense formative added).
5　TH: comp. nom. sg. adj. form of μέγας functioning as a fronted
　　pred. adj.; greater than.
6　TH: substantiver and subject of ἐστίν.
7　TH; combined with μείζων makes an emphatic contrast; much
　　greater than.
8　TH: substantiver that is in contrast to ὁ ἐν ὑμῖν; the one in the
　　world.
9　MH: the root (λαλέω) ends in a vowel, so a connecting vowel
　　will always contract (ε + ου = οῦ).
10　TH: dir. obj. of ἀκούει.
11　TH: ἀκούω can take a gen. case as its dir. obj.
12　TH: substantiver and subject of ἀκούει.
13　TH: forward pointing rel. pron.; the one who.
14　TH: here γινώσκομεν is gapped (implied/elliptical).
15　πλάνη, ης, ἡ, deception, error, fraud.
16　TH: hortatory subj.

ἐκ τοῦ θεοῦ γεγέννηται[1] καὶ γινώσκει τὸν
θεόν. [8] ὁ μὴ ἀγαπῶν οὐκ ἔγνω[2] τὸν θεόν, ὅτι ὁ
θεὸς ἀγάπη[3] ἐστίν. [9] ἐν τούτῳ ἐφανερώθη[4] ἡ
ἀγάπη τοῦ θεοῦ ἐν ἡμῖν, ὅτι τὸν υἱὸν αὐτοῦ
τὸν μονογενῆ[5] ἀπέσταλκεν[6] ὁ θεὸς εἰς τὸν
κόσμον ἵνα ζήσωμεν[7] δι᾽ αὐτοῦ. [10] ἐν τούτῳ
ἐστὶν ἡ ἀγάπη, οὐχ[8] ὅτι ἡμεῖς ⌜ἠγαπήκαμεν[9]
τὸν θεόν, ἀλλ᾽ ὅτι αὐτὸς ἠγάπησεν[10] ἡμᾶς καὶ
ἀπέστειλεν[11] τὸν υἱὸν αὐτοῦ ἱλασμὸν[12] περὶ τῶν

---

1   MH: pf. stem of γεννάω = γεννα (root) › γεγεννα (redupl. γ +
    ε) › γεγεννη (final vowel lengthens).
2   MH: pf. stem of γινώσκω = γνο (root) › ἐγνο (init. consonant
    groups redupl. by adding ε) › ἐγνω (final vowel lengthens).
3   TH: pred. nom.
4   φανερόω, I make manifest, make known.
5   μονογενής, ές, single, only, unique. TH: attrib. adj. in the
    external (2nd attrib.) position.
6   MH: pf. stem of ἀποστέλλω = ἀπο + στελ (root) › ἀπ᾽ (final
    vowel drops off; apocope) + εστελ (vocalic redupl.) ›
    ἀπεσταλ (ε › α; qualitative vowel gradation) › ἀπεσταλκ (pf.
    tense formative added); occurs twice in 1Jn 4.
7   MH: aor. act. subj. 1st pl. of ζάω = ζα (root) › ζη (final vowel
    lengthens) › ζησα (aor. tense formative added) + ωμεν (subj. 1st
    pl. ending) › ζήσωμεν (α + ω = ω; vowels contract).
8   TH: negating the gapped (implied/elliptical) ἐστίν.
9   MH: pf. stem of ἀγαπάω = αγαπα (root) › ἠγαπα (redupl. α
    lengthens to η) › ἠγαπη (final vowel lengthens) › ἠγαπηκ (pf.
    tense formative added).
10 MH: aor. act. indic. 3rd sg. of ἀγαπάω = αγαπα (root) › ἠγαπα
    (hist. aug. added; ε + α = η) › ἠγαπη (final vowel lengthens)
    › ἠγαπησα (aor. tense formative) › ἠγαπησεν (σα › σε in 3rd
    sg.; has a moveable nu).
11 MH: aor. indic. stem of ἀποστέλλω = ἀπο + στελ (root) › ἀπ᾽
    (final vowel drops off; apocope) + εστελ (hist. aug. added) ›
    ἀπεστειλ (ε lengthens to ει; quantitative vowel gradation);
    occurs 3 times in 1Jn 4.
12 ἱλασμός, οῦ, ὁ, expiation, means of atonement. TH: obj.
    complement in a double acc. constr. with τὸν υἱὸν αὐτοῦ as
    the obj.

ἁμαρτιῶν ἡμῶν. ¹¹ ἀγαπητοί, εἰ οὕτως ὁ θεὸς ἠγάπησεν ἡμᾶς, καὶ ἡμεῖς ὀφείλομεν¹ ἀλλήλους ἀγαπᾶν.² ¹² θεὸν οὐδεὶς πώποτε³ τεθέαται·⁴ ἐὰν⁵ ἀγαπῶμεν ἀλλήλους, ὁ θεὸς ἐν ἡμῖν μένει καὶ ἡ ἀγάπη αὐτοῦ ʿἐν ἡμῖν τετελειωμένη⁶ ἐστιν⁾. ¹³ Ἐν τούτῳ γινώσκομεν ὅτι ἐν αὐτῷ μένομεν καὶ αὐτὸς ἐν ἡμῖν, ὅτι ἐκ τοῦ πνεύματος αὐτοῦ δέδωκεν⁷ ἡμῖν. ¹⁴ καὶ ἡμεῖς τεθεάμεθα⁴ καὶ μαρτυροῦμεν ὅτι ὁ πατὴρ ἀπέσταλκεν τὸν υἱὸν σωτῆρα⁸ τοῦ κόσμου. ¹⁵ ὃς ʿἐὰν⁹ ὁμολογήσῃ¹⁰ ὅτι¹¹ ʿἸησοῦς ἐστιν ὁ υἱὸς τοῦ θεοῦ, ὁ θεὸς ἐν αὐτῷ μένει καὶ αὐτὸς¹² ἐν τῷ θεῷ. ¹⁶ καὶ ἡμεῖς ἐγνώκαμεν¹³ καὶ πεπιστεύκαμεν τὴν ἀγάπην ἣν ἔχει ὁ θεὸς ἐν ἡμῖν.

1　ὀφείλω, *I owe, am obligated;* (+inf) *I ought.*

2　TH: complement of ὀφείλομεν. MH pres. act. inf of ἀγαπάω = ἀγαπα (pres. stem) + εν (act. inf. ending) › ἀγαπᾶν (α + ε = ᾶ; contaction); occurs twice in 1Jn 4.

3　πώποτε, *yet, ever, at any point.*

4　θεάομαι, *I observe, behold.* MH: pf. stem = θέα (root) › τεθεα (redupl. θ + ε; θ deaspirates to τ).

5　TH: protasis of a pres. general condition.

6　τελειόω, *I complete, perfect.* TH: periphr. (pf. prtc. + pres. εἰμί = pf. tense), periphr. constr. = pf. mid./pass. indic. 3ʳᵈ sg.

7　MH: pf. stem of δίδωμι = δο (root) › δεδο (redupl. δ + ε) › δεδω (final vowel lengthens) › δεδωκ (pf. tense formative added).

8　σωτήρ, ῆρος, ὁ, *savior, champion, preserver.* TH: obj. complement in a double acc. constr. with τὸν υἱόν as the obj.

9　TH: protasis of a pres. general condition; ὃς ἐάν, *whoever.*

10　ὁμολογέω, *I confess, admit* (in public).

11　TH: marks indir. discourse.

12　TH: subject of a gapped (implied/elliptical) μένει.

13　MH: pf. stem of γινώσκω = γνο (root) › ἐγνο (init. consonant groups redupl. by adding ε) › ἐγνω (final vowel lengthens) › ἐγνωκα (pf. tense formative added).

Ὁ θεὸς ἀγάπη ἐστίν, καὶ ὁ μένων ἐν τῇ ἀγάπῃ ἐν τῷ θεῷ μένει καὶ ὁ θεὸς ἐν αὐτῷ ⌜μένει. [17] ἐν τούτῳ τετελείωται[1] ἡ ἀγάπη μεθ᾽ ἡμῶν, ἵνα παρρησίαν[2] ἔχωμεν[3] ἐν τῇ ἡμέρᾳ τῆς κρίσεως,[4] ὅτι καθὼς ἐκεῖνός ἐστιν καὶ ἡμεῖς ἐσμεν ἐν τῷ κόσμῳ τούτῳ. [18] φόβος[5] οὐκ ἔστιν ἐν τῇ ἀγάπῃ, ἀλλ᾽ ἡ τελεία[6] ἀγάπη ἔξω βάλλει τὸν φόβον,[5] ὅτι ὁ φόβος[5] κόλασιν[7] ἔχει, ὁ δὲ φοβούμενος οὐ τετελείωται[1] ἐν τῇ ἀγάπῃ. [19] ἡμεῖς ⌜ἀγαπῶμεν, ὅτι αὐτὸς πρῶτος ἠγάπησεν ἡμᾶς. [20] ἐάν[8] τις εἴπῃ[9] ὅτι[10] Ἀγαπῶ τὸν θεόν, καὶ τὸν ἀδελφὸν αὐτοῦ μισῇ,[11] ψεύστης[12] ἐστίν· ὁ γὰρ μὴ ἀγαπῶν τὸν ἀδελφὸν αὐτοῦ ὃν ἑώρακεν,[13] τὸν θεὸν[14] ὃν οὐχ ἑώρακεν ⌜οὐ δύναται ἀγαπᾶν.[15]

---

1 τελειόω, *I complete, perfect.*
2 παρρησία, ας, ἡ, *boldness, confidence, outspokenness.*
3 MH: subj. mood lengthens connecting vowel (ομεν › ωμεν).
4 κρίσις, εως, ἡ, *judgment, punishment, justice.*
5 φόβος, ου, ὁ, *fear, intimidation, respect.*
6 τέλειος, α, ον, *complete, perfect, genuine.*
7 κόλασις, εως, ἡ, *punishment, correction.*
8 TH: protasis of a pres. general condition.
9 MH: aor. act. subj. 3rd sg. suppl. from λέγω = ϝεπ (suppl. root) › εϝεπ (vocalic redupl.) › εεπ (ϝ drops out) › ειπ (ε + ε = ει) › εἴπῃ (subj. 3rd sg. ending added).
10 TH: marks dir. discourse and not translated; notice capitalized Ἀγαπῶ.
11 μισέω, *I hate, hold in disfavor.*
12 ψεύστης, ου, ὁ, *liar, cheat, fabricator.* TH: pred. nom.
13 MH: pf. stem of ὁράω = ϝορα (root; Smyth §431) › ϝεϝορα (redupl. of ϝ + ε + root) › ἐϝορα (init. ϝ dissim. into a rough breathing mark; Mounce §32.7) › ἑωρα (ϝ elides causing ο to lengthens to ω) › ἑωρακ (κ = pf. tense formative); occurs twice in 1Jn 4.
14 TH: dir. obj. of ἀγαπᾶν.
15 TH: complement of δύναται.

21 καὶ ταύτην τὴν ἐντολὴν ἔχομεν ἀπ' αὐτοῦ, ἵνα ὁ ἀγαπῶν τὸν θεὸν[1] ἀγαπᾷ καὶ[2] τὸν ἀδελφὸν[3] αὐτοῦ.

---

1   TH: dir. obj. of ἀγαπῶν.
2   TH: additive καί; *even, also.*
3   TH: dir. obj. of ἀγαπᾷ.

I JOHN 5

New Vocabulary by Frequency [Chapter, Book, SBLGNT Occurrences]

μαρτυρία, ας, ἡ, *testimony, evidence, declaration* [6, 6, 37]

ἀληθινός, ή, όν, *true, trustworthy, authentic* [3, 4, 28]

ἁμαρτάνω, *I sin, miss the mark* [3, 10, 43]

νικάω, *I win, conquer, overcome* [3, 6, 28]

ἀδικία, ας, ἡ, *wrongdoing, injustice* [1, 2, 25]

αἴτημα, τος, τό, *request, demand, appeal* [1, 1, 3]

ἅπτω, *I ignite, touch, seize* [1, 1, 39]

βαρύς, εῖα, ύ, *heavy, burdensome* [1, 1, 6]

διάνοια, ας, ἡ, *intelligence, thought, purpose* [1, 1, 12]

εἴδωλον, ου, τό, *idol, false god* [1, 1, 11]

ἥκω, *I have come, am here* [1, 1, 27]

κεῖμαι, *I recline, exist* [1, 1, 24]

νίκη, ης, ἡ, *victory, triumph, conquest* [1, 1, 1]

παρρησία, ας, ἡ, *boldness, confidence, outspokenness* [1, 4, 31]

τεκνίον, ου, τό, *child, dear friend* [1, 7, 8]

φυλάσσω, *I guard, protect, obey* [1, 1, 31]

ψεύστης, ου, ὁ, *liar, cheat, fabricator* [1, 5, 10]

5.1 Πᾶς ὁ πιστεύων ὅτι Ἰησοῦς ἐστιν ὁ χριστὸς ἐκ τοῦ θεοῦ γεγέννηται, καὶ πᾶς ὁ ἀγαπῶν τὸν γεννήσαντα ἀγαπᾷ ⌜καὶ¹ τὸν γεγεννημένον ἐξ αὐτοῦ. ² ἐν τούτῳ γινώσκομεν ὅτι ἀγαπῶμεν τὰ τέκνα τοῦ θεοῦ, ὅταν τὸν θεὸν ἀγαπῶμεν καὶ τὰς ἐντολὰς αὐτοῦ ⌜ποιῶμεν· ³ αὕτη γάρ ἐστιν ἡ ἀγάπη² τοῦ θεοῦ ἵνα τὰς ἐντολὰς αὐτοῦ τηρῶμεν, καὶ αἱ ἐντολαὶ αὐτοῦ βαρεῖαι³ οὐκ εἰσίν, ⁴ ὅτι πᾶν τὸ γεγεννημένον ἐκ τοῦ θεοῦ νικᾷ⁴ τὸν κόσμον. καὶ αὕτη ἐστὶν ἡ νίκη⁵ ἡ νικήσασα⁶ τὸν κόσμον, ἡ πίστις ἡμῶν· ⁵ τίς ⌜δέ⁷ ἐστιν⌝ ὁ νικῶν⁸ τὸν κόσμον εἰ μὴ ὁ πιστεύων ὅτι Ἰησοῦς ἐστιν ὁ υἱὸς τοῦ θεοῦ; ⁶ Οὗτός⁹ ἐστιν ὁ ἐλθὼν¹⁰ δι᾽ ὕδατος καὶ αἵματος, Ἰησοῦς Χριστός·¹¹ οὐκ¹² ἐν τῷ ὕδατι

---

1 NA has ἀγαπᾷ [καὶ] τόν.
2 TH: pred. nom. and postcedent to αὕτη.
3 βαρύς, εῖα, ύ, *heavy, burdensome*. TH: pred. adj.
4 νικάω, *I win, conquer, overcome*. MH: pres. act. indic. 3ʳᵈ sg.
   = νικα (pres. stem) + ει (3ʳᵈ sg. ending) › νικᾶι (α + ε = ᾱ) › νικᾷ (ι subscripts).
5 νίκη, ης, ἡ, *victory, triumph, conquest*. TH: pred. nom. and postcedent to αὕτη.
6 νικάω, *I win, conquer, overcome*. MH: aor. stem of νικάω = νικα (root) › νικη (final vowel lengthens) › νικησα (aor. tense formative added).
7 NA has τίς [δέ] ἐστιν.
8 νικάω, *I win, conquer, overcome*.
9 TH: forward pointing to Ἰησοῦς Χριστός.
10 MH: suppl. aor. stem of ἔρχομαι = ἐλευθ (suppl. root) › ἐλθευ (ευ and θ change places; known as metathesis) › ἐλθ (ευ drops out; known as apocope).
11 TH: app. to ὁ ἐλθὼν δι᾽ ὕδατος καὶ αἵματος.
12 TH: negating the gapped (implied/elliptical) ἐλθών.

μόνον ἀλλ' ἐν¹ τῷ ὕδατι καὶ ⌐ἐν¹ τῷ αἵματι·
καὶ τὸ πνεῦμά ἐστιν τὸ μαρτυροῦν, ὅτι τὸ
πνεῦμά ἐστιν ἡ ἀλήθεια. ⁷ ὅτι² τρεῖς εἰσιν οἱ
μαρτυροῦντες, ⁸ τὸ πνεῦμα καὶ τὸ ὕδωρ καὶ
τὸ αἷμα, καὶ οἱ τρεῖς εἰς τὸ ἕν εἰσιν. ⁹ εἰ τὴν
μαρτυρίαν³ τῶν ἀνθρώπων λαμβάνομεν, ἡ
μαρτυρία³ τοῦ θεοῦ μείζων⁴ ἐστίν, ὅτι αὕτη
ἐστὶν ἡ μαρτυρία⁵ τοῦ θεοῦ ⌐ὅτι μεμαρτύρηκεν
περὶ τοῦ υἱοῦ αὐτοῦ. ¹⁰ ὁ πιστεύων εἰς τὸν
υἱὸν τοῦ θεοῦ ἔχει τὴν μαρτυρίαν³ ἐν ⌐αὐτῷ·⁶
ὁ μὴ πιστεύων τῷ θεῷ⁷ ψεύστην⁸ πεποίηκεν
αὐτόν, ὅτι οὐ πεπίστευκεν εἰς τὴν μαρτυρίαν³
ἣν μεμαρτύρηκεν ὁ θεὸς περὶ τοῦ υἱοῦ αὐτοῦ.
¹¹ καὶ αὕτη ἐστὶν ἡ μαρτυρία,⁵ ὅτι ζωὴν αἰώνιον
ἔδωκεν ⌐ὁ θεὸς ἡμῖν⌐, καὶ αὕτη ἡ ζωὴ ἐν τῷ υἱῷ
αὐτοῦ ἐστιν. ¹² ὁ ἔχων τὸν υἱὸν ἔχει τὴν ζωήν· ὁ
μὴ ἔχων τὸν υἱὸν τοῦ θεοῦ τὴν ζωὴν οὐκ ἔχει.

---

1 TH: modifying the gapped (implied/elliptical) ἐλθών.
2 TH: for.
3 μαρτυρία, ας, ἡ, testimony, evidence, declaration.
4 TH: comp. nom. sg. adj. form of μέγας functioning as a fronted
   pred. nom. and modifying a gapped (implied/elliptical) τὴν
   μαρτυρίαν τῶν ἀνθρώπων; greater than the evidence of
   humanity.
5 μαρτυρία, ας, ἡ, testimony, evidence, declaration. TH: pred.
   nom.
6 NA has ἐν ἑαυτῷ; NA²⁸ has ἐν αὐτῷ.
7 TH: dir. obj. of πιστεύων.
8 ψεύστης, ου, ὁ, liar, cheat, fabricator. TH: fronted obj.
   complement in a double acc. constr. with αὐτόν as the obj.

¹³ Ταῦτα ἔγραψα ⌐ὑμῖν ἵνα εἰδῆτε¹ ὅτι ζωὴν ⌐ἔχετε αἰώνιον⌐,² ⌐τοῖς πιστεύουσιν³⌐ εἰς τὸ ὄνομα τοῦ υἱοῦ τοῦ θεοῦ. ¹⁴ καὶ αὕτη ἐστὶν ἡ παρρησία⁴ ἣν ἔχομεν πρὸς αὐτόν, ὅτι ἐάν⁵ τι⁶ αἰτώμεθα κατὰ τὸ θέλημα αὐτοῦ ἀκούει ἡμῶν. ¹⁵ καὶ ἐάν⁵ οἴδαμεν ὅτι ἀκούει ἡμῶν ὃ ⌐ἐάν⁷ αἰτώμεθα, οἴδαμεν ὅτι ἔχομεν τὰ αἰτήματα⁸ ἃ ᾐτήκαμεν⁹ ⌐ἀπ᾽ αὐτοῦ. ¹⁶ ἐάν⁵ τις ἴδῃ¹⁰ τὸν ἀδελφὸν αὐτοῦ ἁμαρτάνοντα¹¹ ἁμαρτίαν μὴ¹² πρὸς θάνατον,¹³ αἰτήσει, καὶ δώσει αὐτῷ ζωήν, τοῖς ἁμαρτάνουσιν¹⁴ μὴ πρὸς θάνατον. ¹³ ἔστιν ἁμαρτία¹⁵ πρὸς θάνατον· οὐ περὶ ἐκείνης¹⁶ λέγω

---

1   MH: pf. act. subj. 2ⁿᵈ pl. of οἶδα = ϝιδ (root) › ϝεϝιδ (redupl.)
    of ϝ + ε) › εϝιδ (init. ϝ drops out; known as aphaeresis) › εἰδ
    (intervocalic ϝ drops out) › εἰδ + ετε (2ⁿᵈ pl. ending) › εἰδῆτε
    (subj. lengthens connecting vowel; ε › η).
2   TH: attrib. modifying the fronted ζωήν.
3   TH: app. to ὑμῖν in the first clause of 1Jn 5:13.
4   παρρησία, ας, ἡ, boldness, confidence, outspokenness. TH:
    pred. nom.
5   TH: protasis of a pres. general condition.
6   TH: dir. obj. of αἰτώμεθα; something, anything.
7   TH: protasis of a pres. general condition; ὃ ἐάν, whatever.
8   αἴτημα, τος, τό, request, demand, appeal.
9   MH: pf. stem of αἰτέω = αιτε (root) › ητε (vocalic redupl.; α ›
    η) › ᾐτε (ι subscripts) › ᾐτη (final vowel lengthens) › ᾐτηκα
    (pf. tense formative added).
10 MH: aor. suppl. of ὁράω = ϝιδ (root) › ἰδ (init. ϝ drops out;
    known as aphaeresis).
11 ἁμαρτάνω, I sin, miss the mark.
12 TH: negating a gapped (implied/elliptical) ἁμαρτάνοντα; or it
    means leading, resulting.
13 TH: μὴ πρὸς θάνατον, not (sinning) to the point of death.
14 ἁμαρτάνω, I sin, miss the mark. TH: app. to αὐτῷ.
15 TH: pred. nom.; (lit.) there exists sin to the point of death,
    (idiomatic) there exists sin that causes death.
16 TH: ἁμαρτία πρὸς θάνατον is the antecedent.

ἵνα¹ ἐρωτήσῃ. ¹⁷ πᾶσα ἀδικία² ἁμαρτία³ ἐστίν, καὶ ἔστιν ἁμαρτία⁴ οὐ πρὸς θάνατον.

¹⁸ Οἴδαμεν ὅτι πᾶς ὁ γεγεννημένος ἐκ τοῦ θεοῦ οὐχ ἁμαρτάνει,⁵ ἀλλ' ὁ γεννηθεὶς ἐκ τοῦ θεοῦ τηρεῖ ⸂αὐτόν,⁶ καὶ ὁ πονηρὸς⁷ οὐχ ἅπτεται⁸ αὐτοῦ. ¹⁹ οἴδαμεν ὅτι ἐκ τοῦ θεοῦ ἐσμεν, καὶ ὁ κόσμος ὅλος⁹ ἐν τῷ πονηρῷ⁷ κεῖται.¹⁰ ²⁰ οἴδαμεν δὲ ὅτι ὁ υἱὸς τοῦ θεοῦ ἥκει,¹¹ καὶ δέδωκεν ἡμῖν διάνοιαν¹² ἵνα ⸂γινώσκωμεν τὸν ἀληθινόν·¹³ καὶ ἐσμὲν ἐν τῷ ἀληθινῷ,¹³ ¹⁴ἐν τῷ υἱῷ αὐτοῦ Ἰησοῦ Χριστῷ. οὗτός ἐστιν ὁ ἀληθινὸς¹⁵ θεὸς καὶ ζωὴ αἰώνιος.¹⁶

---

1   TH: content of λέγω; *I do not say that he should petition concerning that (type of sin)*.
2   ἀδικία, ας, ἡ, *wrongdoing, injustice*.
3   TH: pred. nom.
4   TH: pred. nom.; (lit.) *there exists sin not to the point of death;* (idiomatic) *there exists sin that does not cause death*.
5   ἁμαρτάνω, *I sin, miss the mark*.
6   NA²⁸ has ἑαυτόν.
7   TH: subst. adj.; *the evil one*.
8   ἅπτω, *I ignite, touch, seize; harm*.
9   TH: attrib. adj. denoting quality, so it always appears in the pred. position; *the whole world*.
10 κεῖμαι, *I recline, exist*.
11 ἥκω, *I have come, am here*.
12 διάνοια, ας, ἡ, *intelligence, thought, purpose*.
13 ἀληθινός, ή, όν, *true, trustworthy, authentic*. TH: subst. adj.
14 TH: gapped (implied/elliptical) ἐσμέν or app. to ἐν τῷ ἀλητινῷ.
15 ἀληθινός, ή, όν, *true, trustworthy, authentic*.
16 TH: dual termination adjective modifying ζωή.

21 Τεκνία,¹ φυλάξατε² ἑαυτὰ³ ἀπὸ τῶν ⌜εἰδώλων.⁴

---

1 τεκνίον, ου, τό, *child, dear friend.*
2 φυλάσσω, *I guard, protect, obey.* MH: impv. in context; aor.
   act. impv. 2ⁿᵈ pl. = φυλακ (root) + σα (aor. tense formative) ›
   φυλαξα (κ + ς = ξ; known as affrication) + τε (2ⁿᵈ pl. ending)
   › φυλάξατε.
3 TH: neuter to agree with τεκνία; *yourselves.*
4 εἴδωλον, ου, τό, *idol, false god.*

II John

ΙΩΑΝΝΟΥ Β

II JOHN

New Vocabulary by Frequency [Chapter, Book, SBLGNT Occurrences]

διδαχή, ῆς, ἡ, *teaching, instruction, doctrine* [3,3,30]

ἐκλεκτός, ἡ, όν, *chosen, selected, choice* [2,2,23]

κυρία, ας, ἡ, *lady, mistress* [2,2,2]

πλάνος, ον, *leading astray, deceitful;* (Subst.) *deceiver* [2,2,5]

ἀδελφή, ῆς, ἡ, *sister* [1,1,25]

ἀντίχριστος, ου, ὁ, *False Messiah, Messiah Opposer* [1,1,5]

ἀπολαμβάνω, *I receive, recover, welcome, take away* [1,1,10]

βούλομαι, *I wish, desire, intend* [1,1,37]

ἔλεος, ους, τό, *mercy, compassion, pity* [1,1,27]

ἐλπίζω, *I hope, expect, look for* [1,1,31]

ἐργάζομαι, *I work, do, perform* [1,1,41]

καινός, ἡ, όν, *new, fresh, novel* [1,1,42]

κοινωνέω, *I share, have a share in* [1,1,8]

λίαν, *very, exceedingly* [1,1,12]

μέλας, μέλαινα, μέλαν, *black; ink* [1,1,6]

μισθός, οῦ, ὁ, *wages, pay, reward* [1,1,29]

ὁμολογέω, *I confess, admit (in public)* [1,1,26]

πλήρης, ες, *full, filled, complete* [1,1,16]

προάγω, *I lead, lead forward, go ahead, go before* [1,1,20]

χάρτης, ου, ὁ, *papyrus, paper* [1,1,1]

ΙΩΑΝΝΟΥ Β

^{1.1} Ὁ πρεσβύτερος ἐκλεκτῇ¹ κυρίᾳ² καὶ τοῖς τέκνοις αὐτῆς, οὓς ἐγὼ ἀγαπῶ ἐν ἀληθείᾳ, καὶ οὐκ ἐγὼ μόνος ἀλλὰ καὶ³ πάντες οἱ ἐγνωκότες⁴ τὴν ἀλήθειαν, ² διὰ τὴν ἀλήθειαν τὴν μένουσαν ἐν ἡμῖν,⁵ καὶ μεθ' ἡμῶν ἔσται⁶ εἰς τὸν αἰῶνα· ³ ἔσται⁷ μεθ' ἡμῶν χάρις⁸ ἔλεος⁹ εἰρήνη παρὰ θεοῦ πατρός, καὶ ⌜παρὰ Ἰησοῦ Χριστοῦ τοῦ υἱοῦ τοῦ πατρός,¹⁰ ἐν ἀληθείᾳ καὶ ἀγάπῃ.

⁴ Ἐχάρην¹¹ λίαν¹² ὅτι εὕρηκα¹³ ἐκ τῶν τέκνων

---

1   ἐκλεκτός, ή, όν, *chosen, selected, choice.*
2   κυρία, ας, ή, *lady, mistress.* TH: here supply *writing to*
3   TH: καί is additive and points to a continuing elliptical statment where here πάντες...ἀλήθειαν is the subject and the verb ἀγαπάω is once more implied; *also.*
4   MH: pf. act. prtc. masc. pl. nom. of γνώσκω = γνο (root) ›› ἐγνο (init. consonant groups redupl. by adding ε) › ἐγνω (final vowel lengthens) › ἐγνωκ (κ pf. tense formative added) › ἐγνωκοτ (οτ is pf. act. prtc. morpheme) › ἐγνωκοτες (ες is nom. pl. masc. ending).
5   TH: διὰ...ἡμῖν is an extended prep. phrase with both τὴν μένουσαν and ἐν ἡμῖν modifying τὴν ἀλήθειαν, *because of the truth that abides in us.*
6   TH: the subject of ἔσται is understood to be τὴν ἀλήθειαν.
7   TH: imperatival future; *May* (subject) *be...*
8   TH: χάρις ... εἰρήνη, These three nom. nouns are subjects of ἔσται.
9   ἔλεος, ους, τό, *mercy, compassion, pity.*
10 TH: τοῦ υἱοῦ τοῦ πατρός, app. phrase further describing Ἰησοῦ Χριστοῦ.
11 MH: aor. pass. indic. 1ˢᵗ sg. of χαίρω = χαρ (root) › ἐχαρ (ε is the hist. aug.) › ἐχαρη (η is the 2ⁿᵈ aor. pass. morpheme) › ἐχάρην (ν is the 1ˢᵗ sg. ending).
12 λίαν, *very, exceedingly.*
13 MH: pf. stem of εὑρίσκω = ευρ (root) › ευρη (η inserted before tense formative in some pf. tense verbs.) › ευρηκα (κα is pf. tense formative)

σου περιπατοῦντας¹ ἐν ἀληθείᾳ, καθὼς ἐντολὴν
ἐλάβομεν² παρὰ τοῦ πατρός. ⁵ καὶ νῦν ἐρωτῶ
σε, κυρία³, οὐχ ὡς ἐντολὴν ˻καινὴν⁴ γράφων σοι˺
ἀλλὰ ἣν⁵ εἴχομεν⁶ ἀπ' ἀρχῆς, ἵνα⁷ ἀγαπῶμεν
ἀλλήλους. ⁶ καὶ αὕτη ἐστὶν ἡ ἀγάπη, ἵνα⁷
περιπατῶμεν κατὰ τὰς ἐντολὰς αὐτοῦ· αὕτη
˻ἡ ἐντολή ἐστιν˺, καθὼς ἠκούσατε ἀπ' ἀρχῆς,
ἵνα ἐν αὐτῇ περιπατῆτε. ⁷ ὅτι πολλοὶ πλάνοι⁸
˻ἐξῆλθον⁹ εἰς τὸν κόσμον, οἱ μὴ ὁμολογοῦντες¹⁰
Ἰησοῦν Χριστὸν ἐρχόμενον ἐν σαρκί· οὗτός
ἐστιν ὁ πλάνος⁸ καὶ ὁ ἀντίχριστος.¹¹ ⁸ βλέπετε¹²
ἑαυτούς, ἵνα μὴ ˻ἀπολέσητε¹³ ἃ ˻εἰργασάμεθα,¹⁴

1   TH: ἐκ τῶν τέκνων σου περιπατοῦντας is a partitive constr.;
     some of your children walking.
2   MH: aor. act. indic. 1ˢᵗ pl. of λαμβάνω.
3   κυρία, ας, ἡ, *lady, mistress*; TH: here a voc. surrounded by
     commas.
4   καινός, ή, όν, *new, fresh, novel.*
5   TH: ἥν, acc. rel. pron., contrasts with ἐντολὴν καινὴν; **the one.**
6   MH: impf. act. indic. 1st pl. of ἔχω = ε + ἐχ (pres. stem) › εἴχ
     (vowels contract; ε + ε = ει) › εἴχ + ο (thematic vowel) + μεν
     (2ⁿᵈ pl. ending) › εἴχομεν.
7   TH: epexegetical ἵνα; *that* (with the sense of *namely that*).
8   πλάνος, ον, *leading astray, deceitful;* (Subst.) *deceiver.*
9   MH: aor. act. indic. 3ʳᵈ pl. of ἐξῆλθον = ελθ (root) › ηλθ
     (temporal aug. ε length. to η) › ἐξ (pref. prep.) + ῆλθ › ἐξῆλθ
     + ον (3ʳᵈ pl. ending) › ἐξῆλθον.
10   ὁμολογέω, *I confess, admit (in public).* TH: app. to πολλοὶ
     πλάνοι.
11   ἀντίχριστος, ου, ὁ, *False Messiah, One opposing the Messiah;*
     Messiah Opposition.
12   TH: indic. and impv. are identical; context suggests impv.
13   MH: aor. act. subj. 2ⁿᵈ plur. of ἀπόλλυμι = ἀπ (pref. prep.) + ολ
     (root) › ἀπολεσα (adds ε before the σα tense formative) + η
     (length. connecting vowel) › ἀπολεση (α absorbed by η) + τε
     (2ⁿᵈ pl. ending) › ἀπολεσητε. TH: *you all might not lose.*
14   ἐργάζομαι, *I work, do, perform.*

ἀλλὰ μισθὸν¹ πλήρη² ⸆ἀπολάβητε.³ ⁹ πᾶς
ὁ ⸆προάγων⁴ καὶ μὴ μένων ἐν τῇ διδαχῇ⁵ τοῦ
Χριστοῦ θεὸν⁶ οὐκ ἔχει· ὁ μένων ἐν τῇ ⸆διδαχῇ,⁵
οὗτος καὶ⁷ τὸν πατέρα καὶ τὸν υἱὸν ἔχει. ¹⁰ εἴ
τις ἔρχεται πρὸς ὑμᾶς καὶ ταύτην τὴν διδαχὴν⁵
οὐ φέρει, μὴ λαμβάνετε⁸ αὐτὸν εἰς οἰκίαν καὶ
χαίρειν⁹ αὐτῷ μὴ λέγετε· ¹¹ ὁ λέγων γὰρ⸍ αὐτῷ
χαίρειν¹⁰ κοινωνεῖ¹¹ τοῖς ἔργοις αὐτοῦ τοῖς
πονηροῖς.¹²

¹² Πολλὰ ἔχων¹³ ὑμῖν γράφειν οὐκ ἐβουλήθην¹⁴
διὰ χάρτου¹⁵ καὶ μέλανος,¹⁶ ἀλλὰ ἐλπίζω¹⁷
⸆γενέσθαι πρὸς ὑμᾶς καὶ στόμα¹⁸ πρὸς στόμα

---

1   μισθός, οῦ, ὁ, wages, pay, reward.
2   πλήρης, ες, full, filled, complete.
3   ἀπολαμβάνω, I receive, recover, welcome, take away.
4   προάγω, I lead, lead forward, go ahead, go before.
5   διδαχή, ῆς, ἡ, teaching, instruction, doctrine.
6   TH: θεὸν οὐκ ἔχει is the main clause; does not have God.
7   TH: καί...καί, translated as both....and.
8   TH: parsed either pres. indic. or pres. impv., but the μή negation
    indicates non-indicative mood.
9   TH: χαίρειν αὐτῷ μὴ λέγετε; Do not say "Greetings" to him.
10 TH: ὁ λέγων γὰρ αὐτῷ χαίρειν; For the one who says
    "Greetings" to him.
11 κοινωνέω, I share, have a share in.
12 TH: external attrib. slot (2ⁿᵈ attrib. position) with τοῖς ἔργοις;
    his evil deeds.
13 TH: concessive adv. prtc.; Although I have much to write to you..
14 βούλομαι, I wish, desire, intend. TH: here γράφειν is elliptical.
15 χάρτης, ου, ὁ, papyrus, paper.
16 μέλας, μέλαινα, μέλαν, black; ink.
17 ἐλπίζω, I hope, expect, look for.
18 TH: στόμα πρὸς στόμα, (lit.) mouth to mouth; (idiomatic) in
    person.

λαλῆσαι, ἵνα ἡ χαρὰ ⌐ὑμῶν¹ ⌐πεπληρωμένη ᾖ⌐.² **13**
Ἀσπάζεταί σε τὰ τέκνα τῆς ἀδελφῆς³ σου τῆς
⌐ἐκλεκτῆς.⁴

---

1 NA has ἡμῶν.
2 MH: pf. stem of πληρόω = πληρο (root) › πληρωμεν (o length.
before mid./pass. tense formative) › πεπληρωμένη (nom. fem
sg. ending). TH: ᾖ πεπληρωμένη is a periphr. constr. (pres.
εἰμί + pf. prtc. = pf. tense) parsed pf. mid./pass. subj. 3ʳᵈ sg.;
(subject) *might be made full*.
3 ἀδελφή, ῆς, ἡ, *sister*.
4 ἐκλεκτός, ἡ, όν, *chosen, selected, choice*. TH: external attrib.
slot (2ⁿᵈ attrib. position) with τῆς ἀδελφῆς; *your chosen sister*.

III John

ΙΩΑΝΝΟΥ Γ

III JOHN

New Vocabulary by Frequency [Chapter, Book, SBLGNT Occurrences]

ἐπιδέχομαι, *I receive, welcome, accept* [2,2,2]

εὐοδόω, *I prosper, succeed, help on the way* [2,2,4]

φίλος, η, ον, *beloved, dear, loving, devoted;* (Subst.) *friend* [2,2,29]

ἀγαθοποιέω, *I do good, do what is right, am helpful* [1,1,10]

ἀληθής, ές, *true, honest, real* [1,1,26]

ἀξίως, *worthily, rightly* [1,1,41]

ἀρκέω, *I am enough, satisfied, content* [1,1,8]

βούλομαι, *I wish, desire, intend* [1,1,37]

Γάϊος, ου, ὁ, *Gaius* [1,1,5]

Διοτρέφης, ους, ὁ, *Diotrephes* [1,1,1]

Δημήτριος , ου, ὁ, *Demetrius* [1,1,3]

ἐθνικός, ή, όν, *unbelieving, worldly;* (Subst.) *Gentile* [1,1,4]

ἐλπίζω, *I hope, expect, look for* [1,1,31]

ἐργάζομαι, *I work, do, perform* [1,1,41]

εὐθέως, *immediately, at once* [1,1,35]

εὔχομαι, *I pray, wish* [1,1,7]

κακοποιέω, *I do wrong, am criminal, harm, injure* [1,1,4]

κάλαμος, ου, ὁ, *reed, staff* [1,1,12]

καλῶς, *well, rightly, fitly, in the right way* [1,1,37]

κωλύω, *I hinder, prevent, deny, withhold* [1,1,23]

λίαν, *very, exceedingly* [1,1,12]

μαρτυρία, ας, ἡ, *testimony, evidence, declaration* [1,1,37]

μέλας, μέλαινα, μέλαν, *black; ink* [1,1,6]

μιμέομαι, *I imitate, portray* [1,1,4]

ξένος, η, ον, *strange;* (Subst.) *stranger, host* [1,1,14]

ὀφείλω, *I owe, am obligated;* (+inf) *I ought* [1,1,35]

προπέμπω, *I accompany, escort, send on one's way* [1,1,9]

ὑγιαίνω, *I am healthy, sound, correct* [1,1,12]

ὑπολαμβάνω, *I take up, assume, believe, reply* [1,1,5]

ὑπομιμνήσκω, *I remember, remind, bring up* [1,1,7]

συνεργός, όν, *helping;* (Subst.) *helper, fellow-worker* [1,1,13]

φιλοπρωτεύω, *I love to be first, wish to be leader* [1,1,1]

φλυαρέω, *I belittle, talk non-sense (about)* [1,1,1]

ΙΩΑΝΝΟΥ Γ

1.1 Ὁ πρεσβύτερος Γαΐῳ¹ τῷ ἀγαπητῷ, ὃν ἐγὼ ἀγαπῶ ἐν ἀληθείᾳ.

² Ἀγαπητέ², περὶ πάντων³ εὔχομαί⁴ σε⁵ εὐοδοῦσθαι⁶ καὶ ὑγιαίνειν,⁷ καθὼς εὐοδοῦταί⁶ σου⁸ ἡ ψυχή. **³** ἐχάρην⁹ γὰρ λίαν¹⁰ ἐρχομένων¹¹ ἀδελφῶν καὶ μαρτυρούντων σου¹² τῇ ἀληθείᾳ, καθὼς¹³ σὺ¹⁴ ἐν ἀληθείᾳ περιπατεῖς. **⁴** μειζοτέραν¹⁵ τούτων οὐκ ἔχω ⌐χαράν, ἵνα¹⁶ ἀκούω τὰ ἐμὰ¹⁷ τέκνα

---

1 Γάϊος, ου, ὁ, *Gaius*.
2 MH: voc. sing. masc. from ἀγαπητός.
3 TH: prep. phrase modifying εὔχομαι, *in all things*.
4 εὔχομαι, *I pray, wish*.
5 TH: σε is the acc. subject of the infinitives εὐοδοῦσθαι and ὑγιαίνειν, together they function as the content of εὔχομαι.
6 εὐοδόω, *I prosper, succeed, help on the way*.
7 ὑγιαίνω, *I am healthy, sound, correct*.
8 TH: σου modifies ἡ ψυχή.
9 MH: aor. pass. indic. 1ˢᵗ sg. of χαίρω = χαρ (root) › ἐχαρ (ε is the hist. aug.) › ἐχαρη (η is the 2ⁿᵈ aor. pass. morpheme) › ἐχάρην (ν is the 1ˢᵗ sg. ending).
10 λίαν, *very, exceedingly*.
11 TH: ἐρχομένων ἀδελφῶν καὶ μαρτυρούντων, gen. abs. constr.
12 TH: σου modifies τῇ ἀληθείᾳ.
13 TH: καθώς sets up the content of μαρτυρούντων; *how, namely how*.
14 TH: emphatic pronoun.
15 MH: fronted comparative adj., typical comparative form of μέγας is μείζων, here –τερος ending (rather than –ων) is used to clarify comparison.
16 TH: epexegetical ἵνα, the content that follows particularizes the preceding τούτων; *that*.
17 TH: from ἐμός, possessive adj.; *my*.

ἐν ⌜τῇ ἀληθείᾳ περιπατοῦντα.¹

⁵ Ἀγαπητέ,² πιστὸν³ ποιεῖς ὃ ἐάν⁴ ἐργάσῃ⁵
εἰς τοὺς ἀδελφοὺς καὶ⁶ ⌜τοῦτο⁷ ξένους,⁸ ⁶ οἳ
ἐμαρτύρησάν σου⁹ τῇ ἀγάπῃ ἐνώπιον ἐκκλησίας,
οὓς καλῶς¹⁰ ποιήσεις προπέμψας¹¹ ἀξίως¹² τοῦ
θεοῦ· ⁷ ὑπὲρ γὰρ τοῦ ὀνόματος ἐξῆλθον μηδὲν¹³
λαμβάνοντες ἀπὸ τῶν ⌜ἐθνικῶν.¹⁴ ⁸ ἡμεῖς¹⁵ οὖν
ὀφείλομεν¹⁶ ⌜ὑπολαμβάνειν¹⁷ τοὺς τοιούτους, ἵνα

---

1   TH: pres. act. prtc. acc. pl. neut. of περιπατέω = περι (pref.
    prep.) + πατε (root) › περιπατου (ε stem vowel contracts
    with o connecting vowel) › περιπατοῦντ (ντ act. prtc.
    morpheme) › περιπατοῦντα (α is acc. pl. neut ending).
2   MH: voc. sing. masc. from ἀγαπητός.
3   TH: fronted object of ποιεῖς.
4   TH: ὃ ἐάν introduces indef. rel. clause; *whatever.*
5   ἐργάζομαι, *I work, do, perform.* MH: aor. act. subj. 2ⁿᵈ sg. of
    ἐργάζομαι = ϝεργαδ (root) › εργαδ (initial ϝ no longer in
    use) + σα (aor. tense formative) › εργασα (final δ of stem
    assimilates to σ due to the aor. tense formative resulting in
    σσ known as geminate σ, then the geminate σ simplifies to
    σ) › εργαση (α absorbed by η the length. connecting vowel)
    › ἐργάσῃ (η + σαι › ηαι, intervocalic sigma elides, ηαι › η, η
    and α contract and the ι subscripts).
6   TH: intensive use of καί; *even though.*
7   TH: likely ellipsis after τοῦτο, supply *are.*
8   ξένος, η, ον, *strange;* (Subst.) *stranger, host.*
9   TH: σου modifies τῇ ἀγάπῃ.
10 καλῶς, *well, rightly, fitly, in the right way.*
11 προπέμπω, *I accompany, escort, send on one's way.* MH:
    aor. act. prtc. nom. sing. masc = προ (pref. prep.) + πεμπ
    (root) › προπεμπσα (aor. tense formative) › προπεμψα (π +
    ς coalesce to ψ) › προπεμψαντς (ντ prtc. morpheme and ς
    ending) › προπέμψας (ντ drops out when followed by ς).
12 ἀξίως, *worthily, rightly.*
13 TH: fronted object.
14 ἐθνικός, ή, όν, *unbelieving, worldly;* (Subst.) *Gentile.*
15 TH: emphatic pronoun.
16 ὀφείλω, *I owe, am obligated;* (+inf) *I ought.*
17 ὑπολαμβάνω, *I take up, assume, believe, reply.*

συνεργοὶ¹ γινώμεθα τῇ ἀληθείᾳ.

⁹ Ἔγραψά ⌐τι τῇ ἐκκλησίᾳ· ἀλλ' ὁ φιλοπρωτεύων² αὐτῶν Διοτρέφης³ οὐκ ἐπιδέχεται⁴ ἡμᾶς. ¹⁰ διὰ τοῦτο, ἐάν⁵ ἔλθω, ὑπομνήσω⁶ αὐτοῦ τὰ ἔργα ἃ ποιεῖ, λόγοις⁷ πονηροῖς φλυαρῶν⁸ ἡμᾶς, καὶ μὴ ἀρκούμενος⁹ ἐπὶ τούτοις οὔτε¹⁰ αὐτὸς¹¹ ἐπιδέχεται¹² τοὺς ἀδελφοὺς καὶ τοὺς βουλομένους¹³ κωλύει¹⁴ καὶ ἐκ τῆς ἐκκλησίας ἐκβάλλει.

¹¹ Ἀγαπητέ, μὴ μιμοῦ¹⁵ τὸ κακὸν ἀλλὰ τὸ

---

1 συνεργός, όν, *helping;* (Subst.) *helper, fellow-worker.* TH: fronted predicate nom.

2 φιλοπρωτεύω, *I love to be first, wish to be leader.* TH: pres. act. prtc. functioning as attrib. modifier in the internal attrib. slot (1st attrib. possition) btw. ὁ and Διοτρέφης.

3 Διοτρέφης, ους, ὁ, *Diotrephes.*

4 ἐπιδέχομαι, *I receive, welcome, accept.*

5 TH: ἐάν + subj. in protasis with fut. tense in apodosis makes a fut. more vivid conditional clause.

6 ὑπομιμνήσκω, *I remember, remind, bring up.* MH: fut. act. indic. 1ˢᵗ sg. of ὑπομιμνήσκω = ὑπο (pref. prep.) + μνη (root) › ὑπομηνς (σ fut. tense formative) › ὑπομνήσω (ω is prim. act. 1ˢᵗ sing. ending.).

7 TH: fronted object of φλυαρῶν.

8 φλυαρέω, *I belittle, talk non-sense (about).*

9 ἀρκέω, *I am enough, satisfied, content.* TH: fronted adv. part. modifying ἐπιδέχεται.

10 TH: οὔτε αὐτὸς ἐπιδέχεται develops previous indictment of verse 9.

11 TH: emphatic pronoun.

12 ἐπιδέχομαι, *I receive, welcome, accept.*

13 βούλομαι, *I wish, desire, intend.* TH: fronted dir. obj. of both κωλύει and ἐκβάλλει.

14 κωλύω, *I hinder, prevent, deny, withhold.*

15 μιμέομαι, *I imitate, portray.* MH: pres. dep. impv. 2ⁿᵈ sing. of μιμέομαι = μιμ (root) › μιμε (connecting vowel) › μιμεσο (2ⁿᵈ sing mid./pass. ending) › μιμοῦ (intervocalic sigma drops out and ε and ο contract to ου).

ἀγαθόν. ὁ ἀγαθοποιῶν¹ ἐκ τοῦ θεοῦ ἐστιν· ὁ
κακοποιῶν² οὐχ ἑώρακεν³ τὸν θεόν. ¹²Δημητρίῳ⁴
μεμαρτύρηται⁵ ὑπὸ πάντων⁶ καὶ ὑπὸ αὐτῆς⁷
τῆς ἀληθείας· καὶ⁸ ἡμεῖς⁹ δὲ μαρτυροῦμεν, καὶ
⌜οἶδας ὅτι ἡ μαρτυρία¹⁰ ἡμῶν ἀληθής¹¹ ἐστιν.
¹³ Πολλὰ¹² εἶχον¹³ ⌜γράψαι σοι⌝, ἀλλ᾽ οὐ
θέλω διὰ μέλανος¹⁴ καὶ καλάμου¹⁵ σοι ⌜γράφειν·

---

1 ἀγαθοποιέω, *I do good, do what is right, am helpful.*
2 κακοποιέω, *I do wrong, am criminal, harm, injure.*
3 MH: pf. stem of ὁράω = ϝορα (root; Smyth §431) › ϝεϝορα
   (redupl. of ϝ + ε + root) › ἑϝορα (init. ϝ dissim. into a rough
   breathing mark; Mounce §32.7) › ἑωρα (ϝ elides causing ο to
   lengthens to ω) › ἑωρακ (κ = pf. tense formative).
4 Δημήτριος , ου, ὁ, *Demetrius.* TH: fronted and dat. of
   advantage; *for, on behalf of, for the benefit of.*
5 MH: pf. mid./pass. indic. 3ʳᵈ sg. of μαρτυρέω = μαρτυρε (root) ›
   μεμαρτυρε (pf. reduplication) › μεμαρτυρη (stems ending in ε
   frequently length. in pf. tense) › μεμαρτύρηται (3rd sg. mid./
   pass. ending).
6 TH: agent of μεμαρτύρηται along with ὑπὸ αὐτῆς τῆς
   ἀληθείας; (lit.) *it has been witnessed by everyone and the
   truth itself.*
7 TH: intensive use of αὐτός; *itself.*
8 TH: additive καί; *also.*
9 TH: emphatic pronoun.
10 μαρτυρία, ας, ἡ, *testimony, evidence, declaration.*
11 ἀληθής, ές, *true, honest, real.*
12 TH: fronted object of εἶχον.
13 TH: imp. act. indic. 1ˢᵗ sg. of ἔχω = σεχ (root) › εεχ (original
   σ drops out but aug. added as if ς was still present) › ειχ (εε
   contract to ει) › ειχον (ο connecting vowel and 1ˢᵗ sg. hist. act.
   ending).
14 μέλας, μέλαινα, μέλαν, *black; ink.*
15 κάλαμος, ου, ὁ, *reed, staff.*

¹⁴ ἐλπίζω¹ δὲ εὐθέως² ‛σε ἰδεῖν›,³ καὶ στόμα⁴ πρὸς στόμα λαλήσομεν.

¹⁵ Εἰρήνη σοι. ἀσπάζονταί σε οἱ φίλοι.⁵ ἀσπάζου⁶ τοὺς φίλους⁵ κατ᾽ ὄνομα.

---

1   ἐλπίζω, *I hope, expect, look for.*
2   εὐθέως, *immediately, at once.*
3   MH: aor. act. inf. of ὁράω = ϝιδ (root) › ιδ (ϝ no longer in use)
    › ιδε (ε connecting vowel) › ιδεεν (εν aor. act. inf. ending) ›
    ἰδεῖν (εε contract to ει).
4   TH: στόμα πρὸς στόμα, (lit.) *mouth to mouth*; (idiomatic) *in person.*
5   φίλος, η, ον, *beloved, dear, loving, devoted;* (Subst.) *friend.*
6   TH: pres. mid./pass. impv. 2ⁿᵈ sg. from ἀσπάζομαι.

Appendices

ΙΩΑΝΝΟΥ Α

1:3 καὶ WH Treg NIV] – RP

4 ἡμεῖς WH Treg NIV] ὑμῖν RP

5 ἐν αὐτῷ οὐκ ἔστιν NIV RP] οὐκ ἔστιν ἐν αὐτῷ WH Treg

7 Ἰησοῦ WH Treg NIV] + Χριστοῦ RP

8 οὐκ ἔστιν ἐν ἡμῖν WH NIV RP] ἐν ἡμῖν οὐκ ἔστιν Treg

2:4 ὅτι WH Treg NIV] – RP

6 αὐτὸς WH Treg] + οὕτως NIV RP

7 Ἀγαπητοί WH Treg NIV] Ἀδελφοί RP • ἠκούσατε WH Treg NIV] + ἀπ᾽ ἀρχῆς RP

14 ἔγραψα WH Treg NIV] Γράφω RP

18 ὅτι WH Treg NIV] + ὁ RP

19 ἐξ ἡμῶν ἦσαν WH Treg NIV] ἦσαν ἐξ ἡμῶν RP

20 καὶ Treg NIV RP] – WH • πάντες WH NIV] πάντα Treg RP

23 ὁ ὁμολογῶν … ἔχει WH Treg NIV] – RP

24 ὑμεῖς WH Treg NIV] + οὖν RP

27 μένει ἐν ὑμῖν WH Treg NIV] ἐν ὑμῖν μένει RP
• αὐτοῦ WH Treg NIV] αὐτὸ RP • μένετε WH Treg
NIV] μενεῖτε RP

28 ἐὰν WH Treg NIV] ὅταν RP • σχῶμεν WH Treg
NIV] ἔχῶμεν RP

29 ὅτι WH RP] + καὶ NIV Treg

3:1 καὶ ἐσμέν WH Treg NIV] – RP • ἡμᾶς WH Treg
NIV] ὑμᾶς RP

2 οἴδαμεν WH Treg NIV] + δὲ RP

5 ἁμαρτίας WH Treg NIV] + ἡμῶν RP

13 μὴ WH Treg RP] καὶ μὴ NIV • ἀδελφοί WH Treg
NIV] + μου RP

14 ἀγαπῶν WH Treg NIV] + τὸν ἀδελφόν RP

15 αὐτῷ WH Treg NIV] ἑαυτῷ RP

16 θεῖναι WH Treg NIV] τιθέναι RP

18 Τεκνία WH Treg NIV] + μου RP

19 ἐν WH] καὶ ἐν Treg NIV RP • γνωσόμεθα WH Treg
NIV] γινώσκομεν RP • τὴν καρδίαν WH NIV] τὰς
καρδίας Treg RP

21 μὴ καταγινώσκῃ ἡμῶν Treg] μὴ καταγινώσκῃ
WH; ἡμῶν μὴ καταγινώσκῃ NIV; ἡμῶν μὴ
καταγινώσκῃ ἡμῶν RP

22 **ἐὰν** Treg NIV RP] ἂν WH • **ἀπ'** WH Treg NIV] παρ' RP

23 **πιστεύσωμεν** WH NIV RP] πιστεύωμεν Treg • **ἡμῖν** WH Treg NIV] – RP

4:2 **γινώσκετε** WH Treg NIV] γινώσκεται RP

3 **τὸν** WH Treg NIV] – RP • **Ἰησοῦν** WH Treg NIV] + Χριστὸν ἐν σαρκὶ ἐληλυθότα RP

10 **ἠγαπήκαμεν** WH NIV] ἠγαπήσαμεν Treg RP

12 **ἐν ἡμῖν τετελειωμένη ἐστιν** NIV] τετελειωμένη ἐν ἡμῖν ἐστίν WH Treg; τετελειωμένη ἐστιν ἐν ἡμῖν RP

15 **ἐὰν** WH NIV] ἂν Treg RP • **Ἰησοῦς** Treg NIV RP] +Χριστός WH

16 **μένει** WH NIV RP] – Treg

19 **ἀγαπῶμεν** WH Treg NIV] + αὐτόν RP

20 **οὐ** WH Treg NIV] πῶς RP

5:1 **καὶ** Treg NIV RP] – WH

2 **ποιῶμεν** WH Treg NIV] τηρῶμεν RP

5 **δέ ἐστιν** Treg NIV] ἐστιν δὲ WH; ἐστιν RP

6 **ἐν** WH Treg NIV] – RP

9 **ὅτι** WH Treg NIV] ἤν RP

10 **αὐτῷ** WH] αὐτῷ Treg RP; ἑαυτῷ NIV

11 ὁ **θεὸς ἡμῖν** WH] ἡμῖν ὁ θεὸς Treg NIV RP

13 **ὑμῖν** WH Treg NIV] + τοῖς πιστεύουσιν εἰς τὸ ὄνομα τοῦ υἱοῦ τοῦ θεοῦ RP • **ἔχετε αἰώνιον** WH Treg NIV] αἰώνιον ἔχετε RP • **τοῖς πιστεύουσιν** WH Treg NIV] καὶ ἵνα πιστεύητε RP

15 **ἐὰν** WH NIV RP] ἂν Treg • **ἀπ'** WH Treg NIV] παρ' RP

18 **αὐτόν** WH Treg NIV] ἑαυτόν RP

20 **γινώσκωμεν** NIV RP] γινώσκομεν WH Treg

21 **εἰδώλων** WH Treg NIV] + Ἀμήν RP

ΙΩΑΝΝΟΥ Β

3 **παρὰ** WH Treg NIV] + κυρίου RP

5 **καινὴν γράφων σοι** Treg NIV] γράφων σοι καινὴν WH RP

6 **ἡ ἐντολή ἐστιν** WH Treg NIV] ἐστιν ἡ ἐντολή RP

7 **ἐξῆλθον** WH Treg NIV] εἰσῆλθόν RP

8 **ἀπολέσητε** WH Treg NIV] ἀπολέσωμεν RP
• **εἰργασάμεθα** WH RP NA] εἰργάσασθε Treg NIV
• **ἀπολάβητε** WH Treg NIV] ἀπολάβωμεν RP

9 **προάγων** WH Treg NIV] παραβαίνων RP • **διδαχῇ** WH Treg NIV] + τοῦ Χριστοῦ RP

11 **λέγων γὰρ** WH Treg NIV] γὰρ λέγων RP

12 **γενέσθαι** WH Treg NIV] ἐλθεῖν RP • **ὑμῶν** WH Treg] ἡμῶν NIV RP • **πεπληρωμένη ᾖ** WH NIV] ᾖ πεπληρωμένη Treg RP

13 **ἐκλεκτῆς** WH Treg NIV] + Ἀμήν RP

ΙΩΑΝΝΟΥ Γ

4 **χαράν** Treg NIV RP] χάριν WH • **τῇ** WH Treg NIV] – RP

5 **τοῦτο** WH Treg NIV] εἰς τοὺς RP

7 **ἐθνικῶν** WH Treg NIV] ἐθνῶν RP

8 **ὑπολαμβάνειν** WH Treg NIV] ἀπολαμβάνειν RP

9 **τι** WH Treg NIV] – RP

12 **οἶδας** WH Treg NIV] οἴδατε RP

13 **γράψαι σοι** WH Treg NIV] γράφειν RP • **γράφειν** WH Treg NIV] γράψαι RP

14 **σε ἰδεῖν** WH Treg NIV] ἰδεῖν σε RP

THE SBLGNT IN COMPARISON TO ECM[1]

In the Catholic letters, the SBLGNT differs from the ECM at
39 places. These places and the differences are listed below
for 1-3 John.[2]

Ref.   SBLGNT] ECM

1 John

1:7	ἐὰν δὲ ἐν] ἐὰν • ἐν
2:6	περιπατεῖν] οὕτως περιπατεῖν
2:16	ἀλλὰ] ἀλλ᾽
2:29	ὅτι πᾶς] •ὅτι καὶ• πᾶς
3:13	μὴ θαυμάζετε] •καὶ• μὴ θαυμάζετε
3:19	ἐν τούτῳ] Καὶ ἐν τούτῳ
3:21	μὴ καταγινώσκῃ ἡμῶν] ἡμῶν μὴ καταγινώσκῃ
5:10	αὐτῷ] αὑτῷ
5:11	ὁ θεὸς ἡμῖν] •ἡμῖν ὁ θεός•
5:18	αὐτόν] ἑαυτόν

2 John

12	χαρὰ ὑμῶν] χαρὰ ἡμῶν

---

1   This section has been amended from the SBLGNT, in that it has
only been reproduced as related to 1-3 John. The SBLGNT's "Appendix: The
SBLGNT in Comparison to ECM" contains all 39 differences between the
SBLGNT and ECM.

2   Occasionally the ECM places bold dots around certain readings
in its text. Sometimes the bold dots signal "alternative readings which were
considered of equal value" by the ECM editorial committee, and sometimes
they mark instances where "the reasons for the reading in the primary line
were regarded as superior, but not sufficiently to rule out with complete
confidence the claims of the indicated alternative reading" (ECM, *The Letters
of Peter*, 24*). Whenever the ECM readings given below are marked by bold
dots in the text, these dots have been duplicated (or adapted as necessary) in
the list.

APPENDIX II

19796	ὁ, ἡ, τό	the; (sub.) he, she, thing
8984	καί	and; (adv.) also, even
5569	αὐτός, ἡ, ὁ	he, she, it; (adj.) -self, same
2899	σύ, σοῦ; ὑμεῖς, ὑμῶν	you; you all
2777	δέ	but, rather, and, now
2737	ἐν	(+dat) in, with, among
2582	ἐγώ, (ἐ)μοῦ; ἡμεῖς, ἡμῶν	I; we
2458	εἰμί	I am, exist, happen
2352	λέγω	I say, speak, claim
1857	εἰς	(+acc) to, into
1621	οὐ, οὐκ, οὐχ	not, no
1407	ὅς, ἥ, ὅ	who, which, that
1387	οὗτος, αὕτη, τοῦτο	this; (sub.) he, she, this one
1307	θεός, οῦ, ὁ and ἡ	God, god, divine one
1294	ὅτι	that, because
1243	πᾶς, πᾶσα, πᾶν	every, each, all, whole
1039	γάρ	for, because, since
1038	μή	not, no; (+subj.) in order that…not
913	ἐκ, ἐξ	(+gen) from, out from
911	Ἰησοῦς, οῦ, ὁ	Joshua, Jesus
887	ἐπί	(+gen/dat/acc) on, near, toward
714	κύριος, ου, ὁ	Lord, master, owner
707	ἔχω	I have, am
698	πρός	(+acc) to, toward, with
667	γίνομαι	I am, become, happen
666	διά	(+gen) through; (+acc) because of
663	ἵνα	in order that, so that

645	ἀπό	(+gen) from, away from
638	ἀλλά	but, yet, rather
633	ἔρχομαι	I come, go
568	ποιέω	I make, do
551	τίς, τί	who? which? what?
550	ἄνθρωπος, ου, ὁ	man, human
534	τις, τι	someone, something
528	Χριστός, οῦ, ὁ	Messiah, Anointed One, Christ
504	ὡς	as, like
502	εἰ	if, whether
495	οὖν	therefore, then
470	κατά	(+gen) against, down; (+acc) according to
470	μετά	(+gen) with; (+acc) after, behind
453	ὁράω	I see, perceive, experience
428	ἀκούω	I hear, obey, listen
415	πολύς, πολλή, πολύ	much, many
415	δίδωμι	I give, entrust
413	πατήρ, πατρός, ὁ	father
389	ἡμέρα, ας, ἡ	day, time
379	πνεῦμα, ατος, τό	spirit, breath
375	υἱός, οῦ, ὁ	son
346	ἤ	or, than
344	εἷς, μία, ἕν	one, single
342	ἀδελφός , οῦ, ὁ	brother
332	περί	(+gen) concerning; (+acc) around
330	ἐάν	if, whenever
330	λόγος, ου, ὁ	word, speech, matter
321	ἑαυτοῦ, ῆς, οῦ	himself, herself, itself
320	οἶδα	I know, understand
297	λαλέω	I speak
273	οὐρανός, οῦ, ὁ	sky, heaven
262	μαθητής, οῦ, ὁ	disciple, student

258	λαμβάνω	I take, receive
250	γῆ, γῆς, ἡ	land, earth
243	ἐκεῖνος, η, ο	that; (sub.) he, she, that one
243	μέγας, μεγάλη, μέγα	large, great
242	πίστις, εως, ἡ	belief, faithfulness, trust, fidelity, faith
241	πιστεύω	I believe, trust
233	ἅγιος, ία, ον	holy, pure, devout; (sub.) Saint
232	ἀποκρίνομαι	I answer
229	ὄνομα, ατος, τό	name
227	οὐδείς, οὐδεμία, οὐδέν	no; (sub.) no one, nothing
221	γινώσκω	I know, understand, learn
221	ὑπό	(+gen) by; (+acc) underneath
217	ἐξέρχομαι	I go out, exit
216	ἀνήρ, ἀνδρός, ὁ	man, husband
216	γυνή, αικός, ἡ	woman, wife
213	τέ	and, so
209	δύναμαι	I am able
208	θέλω	I wish, want
207	οὕτω/οὕτως	thus, so
200	ἰδού	Look!, Notice!, See!
195	Ἰουδαῖος, αία, αῖον	Jewish; (sub.) Jew
194	νόμος, ου, ὁ	law, custom
193	εἰσέρχομαι	I go into, enter
193	παρά	(+gen) along side, from; (+dat) beside, near; (+acc) out from, by
192	γράφω	I write
185	κόσμος, ου, ὁ	world, universe, order
182	καθώς	as, just as
178	μέν	however, but, indeed
176	χείρ, χειρός, ἡ	hand
176	εὑρίσκω	I find, discover

175	ἄγγελος, ου, ὁ	messenger, envoy, angel
174	ὄχλος, ου, ὁ	crowd, multitude
172	ἁμαρτία, ίας, ἡ	sin, guilt, failure
170	ἄν	ever [conditional particle, indicates possibility]
169	ἔργον, ου, τό	work, accomplishment
165	δόξα, ης, ἡ	splendor, glory; reputation
163	πόλις, εως, ἡ	town, city
162	βασιλεία, ας, ἡ	kingdom, providence, dominion
160	ἔθνος, ους, τό	nation, culture group, people
159	τότε	at that time, then
158	ἐσθίω	I eat, drink, consume
158	Παῦλος, ου, ὁ	Paul
156	καρδία, ας, ἡ	heart
156	Πέτρος, ου, ὁ	Peter
155	πρῶτος, η, ον	first, most prominent
155	χάρις, ιτος, ἡ	grace, thankfulness, kindness
154	ἄλλος, η, ο	other, another
154	ἵστημι	I set, place, establish
153	πορεύομαι	I go, walk
150	ὑπέρ	(+gen) on behalf of, for; (+acc) over, beyond
148	καλέω	I call, summon, invite
147	σάρξ, σαρκός, ἡ	flesh, muscle, body
145	νῦν	now, currently, presently
145	ἕως	while, until, up to the point of, as far as
144	ὅστις, ἥτις, ὅ τι	whoever, whichever, any one who
144	προφήτης, ου, ὁ	prophet
143	ἐγείρω	I rise, raise
143	ἀγαπάω	I love, adore

143	ἀφίημι	I release, forgive, reprieve; depart
143	οὐδέ	but not, nor, neither
142	λαός, οῦ, ὁ	people, populace, multitude
142	σῶμα, ατος, τό	body
141	πάλιν	again
140	ζάω	I live
139	φωνή, ῆς, ἡ	voice, sound, communication
135	δύο	two
135	ζωή, ῆς, ἡ	life, existence
135	Ἰωάν(ν)ης, ου, ὁ	John
133	βλέπω	I see, observe, notice
131	ἀποστέλλω	I send (off)
129	σύν	(+dat) with, along with
128	ἀμήν	certainly, truly, indeed
128	νεκρός, ά, όν	dead
126	δοῦλος, ου, ὁ	slave, bondservant
123	ὅταν	whenever, when
122	αἰών, ῶνος, ὁ	age, era, lifetime
122	ἀρχιερεύς, έως, ὁ	high priest, chief priest
122	βάλλω	I throw, place
120	θάνατος, ου, ὁ	death
119	δύναμις, εως, ἡ	power, strength, ability
119	παραδίδωμι	I hand over, deliver, grant
118	μένω	I remain, continue
117	ἀπέρχομαι	I depart, go away
117	ζητέω	I seek, search, inquire
116	ἀγάπη, ης, ἡ	love, adoration
115	βασιλεύς, έως, ὁ	king
115	κρίνω	I judge, decide, choose
114	ἐκκλησία, ας, ἡ	assembly, gathering, community, church
114	ἴδιος, ία, ον	one's own
113	μόνος, η, ον	alone, only

113	οἶκος, ου, ὁ	house, dwelling, family
111	ἀποθνῄσκω	I die, perish
111	ὅσος, η, ον	as many as, as much as, as great as
109	ἀλήθεια, ας, ἡ	truth, reality
109	μέλλω	I am about to, intend
109	παρακαλέω	I encourage, call, request
108	ὅλος, η, ον	whole, entire
108	ἀνίστημι	I raise, resurrect, establish
106	σῴζω	I save, rescue, keep safe
106	ὥρα, ας, ἡ	hour, time, period, season
105	πῶς	how?
102	ὅτε	when
102	ψυχή, ῆς, ἡ	soul, life
102	ἐξουσία, ας, ἡ	authority, capability
101	ἀγαθός, ή, όν	good, beneficial
101	αἴρω	I lift up, raise up, take away
101	δεῖ	I must, am required, ought
101	ὁδός, οῦ, ἡ	road, way, path, trip
101	καλός, ή, όν	beautiful, good, noble
100	ἀλλήλων	one another
100	ὀφθαλμός, οῦ,	eye
100	τίθημι	I put, place, lay
99	τέκνον, ου, τό	child
97	ἕτερος, α, ον	other, another
97	Φαρισαῖος, ου, ὁ	Pharisee, Separatist
97	αἷμα, ατος, τό	blood, bloodshed
97	ἄρτος, ου, ὁ	bread, food
97	γεννάω	I beget, give birth, parent
97	διδάσκω	I teach, instruct
95	ἐκεῖ	there
95	περιπατέω	I walk (about), live, behave

95	φοβέω	I fear, respect; I flee frightened
94	ἐνώπιον	before, face to face, in the view of
94	τόπος, ου, ὁ	place, position
93	ἔτι	yet, still, even now
93	οἰκία, ας, ἡ	house, building, family
93	πούς, ποδός, ὁ	foot
91	δικαιοσύνη, ης, ἡ	righteousness, justice
91	εἰρήνη, ης, ἡ	peace, well-being
91	θάλασσα, ης, ἡ	lake, sea
91	κάθημαι	I sit, settle, reside
91	μηδείς, μηδεμία, μηδέν	no, no one, nothing
90	ἀπόλλυμι	ruin, destroy, perish
90	πίπτω	I fall, collapse
89	ἀκολουθέω	I follow, obey
88	ἑπτά	seven
87	οὔτε	and not, nor, neither
86	ἄρχω	I rule, lead, begin
86	πληρόω	I fill, complete, fulfill
85	προσέρχομαι	I go to, visit, approach
85	καιρός, οῦ, ὁ	time, period, season
85	προσεύχομαι	I pray, petition a deity
83	κἀγώ	and I, I too (crasis καὶ ἐγώ)
83	μήτηρ, τρός, ἡ	mother
83	ὥστε	so that, therefore, consequently
82	ἕκαστος, η, ον	every, each
81	ἀναβαίνω	I go up, ascend
81	ὅπου	where, whereas, whenever
81	ἐκβάλλω	I throw out, expel, reject
81	μᾶλλον	more, exceedingly, rather
80	καταβαίνω	I go down, descend
80	Μωϋσῆς, ὁ	Moses

79	ἀπόστολος, ου, ὁ	delegate, ambassador, apostle
79	δίκαιος, αία, ον	just, righteous, fair
79	πέμπω	I send, despatch
79	ὑπάγω	I withdraw, go away
78	πονηρός, ά, όν	evil, bad, worthless, sick
78	στόμα, ατος, τό	mouth, opening
77	ἀνοίγω	I open
77	βαπτίζω	I soak, submerge, wash, baptize
77	Ἰερουσαλήμ, ἡ	Jerusalem
77	σημεῖον, ου, τό	sign, mark, signal, miracle
76	μαρτυρέω	I give evidence, witness, testify
76	πρόσωπον, ου, τό	face, appearance, expression, presence
76	ὕδωρ, ατος, τό	water, rain
75	εὐαγγέλιον, ου, τό	good news, gospel
75	δώδεκα	twelve
75	κεφαλή, ῆς, ἡ	head
75	Σίμων, ωνος, ὁ	Simon
74	ἀποκτείνω, ἀποκτέννω	I kill, slay
74	χαίρω	I am glad, rejoice, welcome
73	Ἀβραάμ, ὁ	Abraham
72	πίνω	I drink
72	φῶς, φωτός, τό	light, torch
72	ἱερόν, οῦ, τό	temple, holy place
71	πῦρ, ός, τό	fire
71	τηρέω	I watch over, guard, keep
70	αἰτέω	I ask, demand
69	αἰώνιος, ον	long-lasting, eternal
69	ἄγω	I lead, carry, arrest, observe
68	ἐμός, ή, όν	my, mine
68	τρεῖς, τρία	three

68	Ἰσραήλ, ὁ	Israel
68	σάββατον, ου, τό	Sabbath
67	ῥῆμα, ατος, τό	word, saying, thing
67	πιστός, ή, όν	faithful, trustworthy, believing
67	πλοῖον, ου, τό	boat, ship, vessel
67	ἀπολύω	I release, pardon, dismiss
66	ἐντολή, ῆς, ἡ	command, order, commandment
66	καρπός, ου, ὁ	fruit, produce, profit
66	πρεσβύτερος, α, ον	aged, old; (Subst.) elder
66	φέρω	I carry, bring, lead
65	φημί	I say, declare
65	εἴτε	if, either, or, whether
63	γραμματεύς, έως, ὁ	scribe, law expert, high official
63	δαιμόνιον, ου, τό	demon, evil spirit, inferior divinity
63	ἐρωτάω	I ask, inquire, question
63	ὄρος, ους, τό	mountain, hill
62	ἔξω	outside, out
62	δοκέω	I think, suppose, form an opinion; I seem, suppose
62	θέλημα, ατος, τό	will, want
62	θρόνος, ου, ὁ	chair, seat, throne
62	Ἱεροσόλυμα, τά	Jerusalem (city or its inhabitants)
61	ἀγαπητός, ή, όν	beloved, dearly loved
61	Γαλιλαία, ας, ἡ	Galilee
61	δοξάζω	I honor, esteem in high regard, exalt, glorify
61	κηρύσσω	I preach, proclaim, announce
61	νύξ, νυκτός, ἡ	night (often metaph.)
61	ὧδε	here, thus, in this way, exceedingly so

60	ἤδη	already, now; by this time
60	ἱμάτιον, ου, τό	garment; outer garment
60	προσκυνέω	I worship, prostrate myself
60	ὑπάρχω	I am present, at one's disposal; I am, exist
59	ἀσπάζομαι	I greet, welcome
59	Δαυίδ, ὁ	David
59	διδάσκαλος, ου, ὁ	teacher, master
59	λίθος, ου, ὁ	stone
59	συνάγω	I gather together, collect; receive as a guest
59	χαρά, ᾶς, ἡ	joy, delight, gladness
59	εὐθύς, εῖα, ύ	immediately, straight, proper
58	θεωρέω	I view (as a spectator), behold, observe, see
58	μέσος, η, ον	middle, in the midst
57	τοιοῦτος, αὑτη, οῦτον	such as this, of such a kind
56	δέχομαι	I take, receive; welcome
56	ἐπερωτάω	I ask, inquire
56	μηδέ	but not, nor; not even, not either
56	συναγωγή, ῆς, ἡ	assembly, gathering; synagogue
56	τρίτος, η, ον	third
55	ἀρχή, ῆς, ἡ	beginning; power; rule
55	κράζω	I call out, cry out, scream
55	λοιπός, ή, όν	rest, remaining; from now on
55	Πιλᾶτος, ου, ὁ	Pilate
54	δεξιός, ά, όν	right (directional; often metph.); true
54	εὐαγγελίζω	I bring/proclaim (the) good news

54	οὐχί	not, no, in no way (intensified οὐ)
53	χρόνος, ου, ὁ	time, occasion
53	διό	therefore, for this reason
53	ἐλπίς, ίδος, ἡ	expectation, hope
53	ὅπως	how; in order that
52	ἐπαγγελία, ας, ἡ	promise, offer
52	ἔσχατος, η, ον	last, farthest, least
52	παιδίον, ου, τό	child; young servant/ slave
52	πείθω	I persuade, win over; depend on
52	σπείρω	I sow seed, scatter
51	σοφία, ας, ἡ	wisdom, sound judgement
50	γλῶσσα, ης, ἡ	tongue; language; joyful speech
50	κακός, ή, όν	evil, bad; incorrect
50	μακάριος, ία, ιον	favored, blessed
50	παραβολή, ῆς, ἡ	parable, illustration; type, embodiment
50	τυφλός, ή, όν	blind (often metaph.)
49	γραφή, ῆς, ἡ	scripture, writing[1]

VOCABULARY SORTED BY FREQUENCY 50 TIMES OR MORE

---

1 Though γραγή occurs 49 times in the SBLGNT, this word occurs 50 times in the NA. As such, many resources include γραφή in their most frequently occurring word list and retention requirements. To retain this standard, it has also been included in this most frequently occurring vocabulary list. Γραγή is not included in the General Reader's footnotes or chapter vocabulary helps.

APPENDIX III

VOCABULARY 50 TIMES OF MORE ARRANGED ALPHABETICALLY

A α

Ἀβραάμ, ὁ	*Abraham*
ἀγαθός, ή, όν	*good, beneficial*
ἀγαπάω	*I love, adore*
ἀγάπη, ης, ἡ	*love, adoration*
ἀγαπητός, ή, όν	*beloved, dearly loved*
ἄγγελος, ου, ὁ	*messenger, envoy, angel*
ἅγιος, ία, ον	*holy, pure, devout; (Subst.) Saint*
ἄγω	*I lead, carry, arrest, observe*
ἀδελφός , οῦ, ὁ	*brother*
αἷμα, ατος, τό	*blood, bloodshed*
αἴρω	*I lift up, raise up, take away*
αἰτέω	*I ask, demand*
αἰών, ῶνος, ὁ	*age, era, lifetime*
αἰώνιος, ον	*long-lasting, eternal*
ἀκολουθέω	*I follow, obey*
ἀκούω	*I hear, obey, listen*
ἀλήθεια, ας, ἡ	*truth, reality*
ἀλλά	*but, yet, rather*
ἀλλήλων	*one another*
ἄλλος, η, ο	*other, another*
ἁμαρτία, ίας, ἡ	*sin, guilt, failure*
ἀμήν	*certainly, truly, indeed*
ἄν	*ever [conditional particle, indicates possibility]*
ἀναβαίνω	*I go up, ascend*
ἀνήρ, ἀνδρός, ὁ	*man, husband*
ἄνθρωπος, ου, ὁ	*man, human*
ἀνίστημι	*I raise, resurrect, establish*
ἀνοίγω	*I open*
ἀπέρχομαι	*I depart, go away*

ἀπό	(+gen) from, away from
ἀποθνήσκω	I die, perish
ἀποκρίνομαι	I answer
ἀποκτείνω, ἀποκτέννω	I kill, slay
ἀπόλλυμι	I ruin, destroy, perish
ἀπολύω	I release, pardon, dismiss
ἀποστέλλω	I send (off)
ἀπόστολος, ου, ὁ	delegate, ambassador, apostle
ἄρτος, ου, ὁ	bread, food
ἀρχή, ῆς, ἡ	beginning; power; rule
ἀρχιερεύς, έως, ὁ	high priest, chief priest
ἄρχω	I rule, lead, begin
ἀσπάζομαι	I greet, welcome
αὐτός, ή, ὁ	he, she, it; (adj.) -self, same
ἀφίημι	I release, forgive, reprieve; depart

Β β

βάλλω	I throw, place
βαπτίζω	I soak, submerge, wash, baptize
βασιλεία, ας, ἡ	kingdom, providence, dominion
βασιλεύς, έως, ὁ	king
βλέπω	I see, observe, notice

Γ γ

Γαλιλαία, ας, ἡ	Galilee
γάρ	for, because, since
γεννάω	I beget, give birth, parent
γῆ, γῆς, ἡ	land, earth
γίνομαι	I am, become, happen
γινώσκω	I know, understand, learn
γλῶσσα, ης, ἡ	tongue; language; joyful speech
γραμματεύς, έως, ὁ	scribe, law expert, high official
γραφή, ῆς, ἡ	scripture, writing

γράφω	*I write*
γυνή, αικός, ἡ	*woman, wife*

Δ δ

δαιμόνιον, ου, τό	*demon, evil spirit, inferior divinity*
Δαυίδ, ὁ	*David*
δέ	*but, rather, and, now*
δεῖ	*I must, am required, ought*
δεξιός, ά, όν	*right (directional; often metph.); true*
δέχομαι	*I take, receive; welcome*
διά	*(+gen) through; (+acc) because of*
διδάσκαλος, ου, ὁ	*teacher, master*
διδάσκω	*I teach, instruct*
δίδωμι	*I give, entrust*
δίκαιος, αία, ον	*just, righteous, fair*
δικαιοσύνη, ης, ἡ	*righteousness, justice*
διό	*therefore, for this reason*
δοκέω	*I think, suppose, form an opinion; I seem, suppose*
δόξα, ης, ἡ	*splendor, glory; reputation*
δοξάζω	*I honor, esteem in high regard, exalt, glorify*
δοῦλος, ου, ὁ	*slave, bondservant*
δύναμαι	*I am able*
δύναμις, εως, ἡ	*power, strength, ability*
δύο	*two*
δώδεκα	*twelve*

E ε

ἐάν	*if, whenever*
ἑαυτοῦ, ῆς, οῦ	*himself, herself, itself*
ἐγείρω	*I rise, raise*

ἐγώ, (ἐ)μοῦ; ἡμεῖς, ἡμῶν	*I; we*
ἔθνος, ους, τό	*nation, culture group, people*
εἰ	*if, whether*
εἰμί	*I am, exist, happen*
εἰρήνη, ης, ἡ	*peace, well-being*
εἷς, μία, ἕν	*one, single*
εἰς	*(+acc) to, into*
εἰσέρχομαι	*I go into, enter*
εἴτε	*if, either, or, whether*
ἐκ, ἐξ	*(+gen) from, out from*
ἕκαστος, η, ον	*every, each*
ἐκβάλλω	*I throw out, expel, reject*
ἐκεῖ	*there*
ἐκεῖνος, η, ο	*that; (Subst.) he, she, that one*
ἐκκλησία, ας, ἡ	*assembly, gathering, community,*
	church
ἐλπίς, ίδος, ἡ	*expectation, hope*
ἐμός, ή, όν	*my, mine*
ἐν	*(+dat) in, with, among*
ἐντολή, ῆς, ἡ	*command, order, commandment*
ἐνώπιον	*before, face to face, in the view of*
ἐξέρχομαι	*I go out, exit*
ἐξουσία, ας, ἡ	*authority, capability*
ἔξω	*outside, out*
ἐπαγγελία, ας, ἡ	*promise, offer*
ἐπερωτάω	*I ask, inquire*
ἐπί	*(+gen/dat/acc) on, near, toward*
ἑπτά	*seven*
ἔργον, ου, τό	*work, accomplishment*
ἔρχομαι	*I come, go*
ἐρωτάω	*I ask, inquire, question*
ἐσθίω	*I eat, drink, consume*
ἔσχατος, η, ον	*last, farthest, least*
ἕτερος, α, ον	*other, another*
ἔτι	*yet, still, even now*
εὐαγγελίζω	*I bring/proclaim (the) good news*
εὐαγγέλιον, ου, τό	*good news, gospel*

εὐθύς, εῖα, ύ	*immediately, straight, proper*
εὑρίσκω	*I find, discover*
ἔχω	*I have, am*
ἕως	*while, until, up to the point of, as far as*

Z ζ

ζάω	*I live*
ζητέω	*I seek, search, inquire*
ζωή, ῆς, ἡ	*life, existence*

H η

ἤ	*or, than*
ἤδη	*already, now; by this time*
ἡμέρα, ας, ἡ	*day, time*

Θ ϑ

θάλασσα, ης, ἡ	*lake, sea*
θάνατος, ου, ὁ	*death*
θέλημα, ατος, τό	*will, want*
θέλω	*I wish, want*
θεός, οῦ, ὁ and ἡ	*God, god, divine one*
θεωρέω	*I view (as a spectator), behold, observe, see*
θρόνος, ου, ὁ	*chair, seat, throne*

I ι

ἴδιος, ία, ον	*one's own*
ἰδού	*Look!, Notice!, See!*

ἱερόν, οῦ, τό	temple, holy place
Ἱεροσόλυμα, τά	Jerusalem (city or its inhabitants)
Ἱερουσαλήμ, ἡ	Jerusalem
Ἰησοῦς, οῦ, ὁ	Joshua, Jesus
ἱμάτιον, ου, τό	garment; outer garment
ἵνα	in order that, so that
Ἰουδαῖος, αία, αῖον	Jewish; (Subst..) Jew
Ἰσραήλ, ὁ	Israel
ἵστημι	I set, place, establish
Ἰωάν(ν)ης, ου, ὁ	John

Κ κ

κἀγώ	and I, I too (crasis καὶ ἐγώ)
κάθημαι	I sit, settle, reside
καθώς	as, just as
καί	and; (adv.) also, even
καιρός, οῦ, ὁ	time, period, season
κακός, ή, όν	evil, bad; incorrect
καλέω	I call, summon, invite
καλός, ή, όν	beautiful, good, noble
καρδία, ας, ἡ	heart
καρπός, ου, ὁ	fruit, produce, profit
κατά	(+gen) against, down; (+acc) according to
καταβαίνω	I go down, descend
κεφαλή, ῆς, ἡ	head
κηρύσσω	I preach, proclaim, announce
κόσμος, ου, ὁ	world, universe, order
κράζω	I call out, cry out, scream
κρίνω	I judge, decide, choose
κύριος, ου, ὁ	Lord, master, owner

Λ λ

λαλέω	*I speak*
λαμβάνω	*I take, receive*
λαός, οῦ, ὁ	*people, populace, multitude*
λέγω	*I say, speak, claim*
λίθος, ου, ὁ	*stone*
λόγος, ου, ὁ	*word, speech, matter*
λοιπός, ή, όν	*rest, remaining; from now on*

M μ

μαθητής, οῦ, ὁ	*disciple, student*
μακάριος, ία, ιον	*favored, blessed*
μᾶλλον	*more, exceedingly, rather*
μαρτυρέω	*I give evidence, witness, testify*
μέγας, μεγάλη, μέγα	*large, great*
μέλλω	*I am about to, intend*
μέν	*however, but, indeed*
μένω	*I remain, continue*
μέσος, η, ον	*middle, in the midst*
μετά	*(+gen) with; (+acc) after, behind*
μή	*not, no; (+subj.) in order that...not*
μηδέ	*but not, nor; not even, not either*
μηδείς, μηδεμία, μηδέν	*no, no one, nothing*
μήτηρ, τρός, ἡ	*mother*
μόνος, η, ον	*alone, only*
Μωϋσῆς, ὁ	*Moses*

N ν

νεκρός, ά, όν	*dead*
νόμος, ου, ὁ	*law, custom*
νῦν	*now, currently, presently*
νύξ, νυκτός, ἡ	*night (often metaph.)*

O o

ὁ, ἡ, τό	*the; (Subst.) he, she, thing*
ὁδός, οῦ, ἡ	*road, way, path, trip*
οἶδα	*I know, understand*
οἰκία, ας, ἡ	*house, building, family*
οἶκος, ου, ὁ	*house, dwelling, family*
ὅλος, η, ον	*whole, entire*
ὄνομα, ατος, τό	*name*
ὅπου	*where, whereas, whenever*
ὅπως	*how; in order that*
ὁράω	*I see, perceive, experience*
ὄρος, ους, τό	*mountain, hill*
ὅς, ἥ, ὅ	*who, which, that*
ὅσος, η, ον	*as many as, as much as, as great as*
ὅστις, ἥτις, ὅ τι	*whoever, whichever, any one who*
ὅταν	*whenever, when*
ὅτε	*when*
ὅτι	*that, because*
οὐ, οὐκ, οὐχ	*not, no*
οὐδέ	*but not, nor, neither*
οὐδείς, οὐδεμία, οὐδέν	*no; (Subst.) no one, nothing*
οὖν	*therefore, then*
οὐρανός, οῦ, ὁ	*sky, heaven*
οὔτε	*and not, nor, neither*
οὗτος, αὕτη, τοῦτο	*this; (Subst.) he, she, this one*
οὕτω/οὕτως	*thus, so*
οὐχί	*not, no, in no way (intensified οὐ)*
ὀφθαλμός, οῦ,	*eye*
ὄχλος, ου, ὁ	*crowd, multitude*

Π π

παιδίον, ου, τό	*child; young servant/slave*
πάλιν	*again*

παρά	*(+gen) along side, from; (+dat) beside, near; (+acc) out from, by*
παραβολή, ῆς, ἡ	*parable, illustration; type, embodiment*
παραδίδωμι	*I hand over, deliver, grant*
παρακαλέω	*I encourage, call, request*
πᾶς, πᾶσα, πᾶν	*every, each, all, whole*
πατήρ, πατρός, ὁ	*father*
Παῦλος, ου, ὁ	*Paul*
πείθω	*I persuade, win over; depend on*
πέμπω	*I send, despatch*
περί	*(+gen) concerning; (+acc) around*
περιπατέω	*I walk (about), live, behave*
Πέτρος, ου, ὁ	*Peter*
Πιλᾶτος, ου, ὁ	*Pilate*
πίνω	*I drink*
πίπτω	*I fall, collapse*
πιστεύω	*I believe, trust*
πίστις, εως, ἡ	*belief, faithfulness, trust, fidelity, faith*
πιστός, ή, όν	*faithful, trustworthy, believing*
πληρόω	*I fill, complete, fulfill*
πλοῖον, ου, τό	*boat, ship, vessel*
πνεῦμα, ατος, τό	*spirit, breath*
ποιέω	*I make, do*
πόλις, εως, ἡ	*town, city*
πολύς, πολλή, πολύ	*much, many*
πονηρός, ά, όν	*evil, bad, worthless, sick*
πορεύομαι	*I go, walk*
πούς, ποδός, ὁ	*foot*
πρεσβύτερος, α, ον	*aged, old;* (Subst.) *elder*
πρός	*(+acc) to, toward, with*
προσέρχομαι	*I go to, visit, approach*
προσεύχομαι	*I pray, petition a deity*
προσκυνέω	*I worship, prostrate myself*
πρόσωπον, ου, τό	*face, appearance, expression, presence*

προφήτης, ου, ὁ	*prophet*
πρῶτος, η, ον	*first, most prominent*
πῦρ, ός, τό	*fire*
πῶς	*how?*

Ρ ρ

ῥῆμα, ατος, τό	*word, saying, thing*

Σ σ

σάββατον, ου, τό	*Sabbath*
σάρξ, σαρκός, ἡ	*flesh, muscle, body*
σημεῖον, ου, τό	*sign, mark, signal, miracle*
Σίμων, ωνος, ὁ	*Simon*
σοφία, ας, ἡ	*wisdom, sound judgement*
σπείρω	*I sow seed, scatter*
στόμα, ατος, τό	*mouth, opening*
σύ, σοῦ; ὑμεῖς, ὑμῶν	*you; you all*
σύν	*(+dat) with, along with*
συνάγω	*I gather together, collect; receive as a guest*
συναγωγή, ῆς, ἡ	*assembly, gathering; synagogue*
σῴζω	*I save, rescue, keep safe*
σῶμα, ατος, τό	*body*

Τ τ

τέ	*and, so*
τέκνον, ου, τό	*child*
τηρέω	*I watch over, guard, keep*
τίθημι	*I put, place, lay*
τις, τι	*someone, something*
τίς, τί	*who? which? what?*
τοιοῦτος, αύτη, οῦτον	*such as this, of such a kind*

τόπος, ου, ὁ	*place, position*
τότε	*at that time, then*
τρεῖς, τρία	*three*
τρίτος, η, ον	*third*
τυφλός, ή, όν	*blind (often metaph.)*

ϒ υ

ὕδωρ, ατος, τό	*water, rain*
υἱός, οῦ, ὁ	*son*
ὑπάγω	*I withdraw, go away*
ὑπάρχω	*I am present, at one's disposal; I am, exist*
ὑπέρ	*(+gen) on behalf of, for; (+acc) over, beyond*
ὑπό	*(+gen) by; (+acc) underneath*

Φ φ

Φαρισαῖος, ου, ὁ	*Pharisee, Separatist*
φέρω	*I carry, bring, lead*
φημί	*I say, declare*
φοβέω	*I fear, respect; I flee frightened*
φωνή, ῆς, ἡ	*voice, sound, communication*
φῶς, φωτός, τό	*light, torch*

Χ χ

χαίρω	*I am glad, rejoice, welcome*
χαρά, ᾶς, ἡ	*joy, delight, gladness*
χάρις, ιτος, ἡ	*grace, thankfulness, kindness*
χείρ, χειρός, ἡ	*hand*
Χριστός, οῦ, ὁ	*Messiah, Anointed One, Christ*
χρόνος, ου, ὁ	*time, occasion,*

Ψ ψ

ψυχή, ῆς, ἡ	*soul, life*

Ω ω

ὧδε	*here, thus, in this way, exceedingly so*
ὥρα, ας, ἡ	*hour, time, period, season*
ὡς	*as, like*
ὥστε	*so that, therefore, consequently*

APPENDIX IV

PARADIGMS

Athematic (μι) Stems: no connecting vowels

	Primary Tense				Secondary/Historical Tense			
	Active		Middle/Passive		Active		Middle/Passive	
	Singular	Plural	Singular	Plural	Singular	Plural	Singular	Plural
1st	μι	μεν	μαι	μεθα	ν	μεν	μην	μεθα
2nd	ς	τε	σαι	σθε	ς	τε	σο	σθε
3rd	σι(ν)	ασι(ν)	ται	νται	_	σαν	το	ντο

Thematic (ω) Stems: connecting vowel included

	Primary Tense				Secondary/Historical Tense			
	Active		Middle/Passive		Active		Middle/Passive	
	Singular	Plural	Singular	Plural	Singular	Plural	Singular	Plural
1st	ω	ομεν	ομαι	ομεθα	ον	ομεν	ομην	ομεθα
2nd	εις	ετε	η	εσθε	ες	ετε	ου	εσθε
3rd	ει	ουσι	εται	ονται	- / ε	ον	ετο	οντο

Imperative (using λύω)

			Active	Middle	Passive
Present	Singular	2nd	λῦε	λύου	
		3rd	λυέτω	λυέσθω	
	Plural	2nd	λύετε	λύεσθε	
		3rd	λυέτωσαν	λυέσθωσαν	
Aorist	Singular	2nd	λῦσον	λῦσαι	λύθητι
		3rd	λυσάτω	λυσάσθω	λυθήτω
	Plural	2nd	λύσατε	λύσασθε	λύθητε
		3rd	λυσάτωσαν	λυσάσθωσαν	λυθήτωσαν

Infinitive (using λύω)

	Active	Middle	Passive
Present	λυείν	λύεσθαι	
Aorist	λῦσαι	λύσασθαι	λυθῆναι
Perfect	λελυκέναι	λελύσθαι	

Participle (using λύω)

			Present		Aorist			Perfect	
			Act.	Mid./Pass.	Act.	Mid.	Pass.	Act.	Mid./Pass.
Masculine	Singular	Nom.	λύων	λυόμενος	λύσας	λυσάμενος	λυθείς	λελυκώς	λελυμένος
		Gen.	λύοντος	λυομένου	λύσαντος	λυσαμένου	λυθέντος	λελυκότος	λελυμένου
		Dat.	λύοντι	λυομένῳ	λύσαντι	λυσαμένῳ	λυθέντι	λελυκότι	λελυμένῳ
		Acc.	λύοντα	λυόμενον	λύσαντα	λυσάμενον	λυθέντα	λελυκότα	λελυμένον
	Plural	Nom.	λύοντες	λυόμενοι	λύσαντες	λυσάμενοι	λυθέντες	λελυκότες	λελυμένοι
		Gen.	λυόντων	λυομένων	λυσάντων	λυσαμένων	λυθέντων	λελυκότων	λελυμένων
		Dat.	λύουσι(ν)	λυομένοις	λύσασι(ν)	λυσαμένοις	λυθεῖσι(ν)	λελυκόσι(ν)	λελυμένοις
		Acc.	λύοντας	λυομένους	λύσαντας	λυσαμένους	λυθέντας	λελυκότας	λελυμένους
Feminine	Singular	Nom.	λύουσα	λυομένη	λύσασα	λυσαμένη	λυθεῖσα	λελυκυῖα	λελυμένη
		Gen.	λυούσης	λυομένης	λυσάσης	λυσαμένης	λυθείσης	λελυκυίας	λελυμένης
		Dat.	λυούσῃ	λυομένῃ	λυσάῃ	λυσαμένῃ	λυθείσῃ	λελυκυίᾳ	λελυμένῃ
		Acc.	λύουσαν	λυομένην	λύσασαν	λυσαμένην	λυθεῖσαν	λελυκυῖαν	λελυμένην
	Plural	Nom.	λύουσαι	λυόμεναι	λύσασαι	λυσάμεναι	λυθεῖσαι	λελυκυῖαι	λελυμέναι
		Gen.	λυουσῶν	λυομένων	λυσασῶν	λυσαμένων	λυθεισῶν	λελυκυιῶν	λελυμένων
		Dat.	λυούσαις	λυομέναις	λυσάσαις	λυσαμέναις	λυθείσαις	λελυκυίαις	λελυμέναις
		Acc.	λυούσας	λυομένας	λυσάσας	λυσαμένας	λυθείσας	λελυκυίας	λελυμένας
Neuter	Singular	Nom.	λῦον	λυόμενον	λῦσαν	λυσάμενον	λυθέν	λελυκός	λελυμένον
		Gen.	λύοντος	λυομένου	λύσαντος	λυσαμένου	λυθέντος	λελυκότος	λελυμένου
		Dat.	λύοντι	λυομένῳ	λύσαντι	λυσαμένῳ	λυθέντι	λελυκότι	λελυμένῳ
		Acc.	λῦον	λυόμενον	λῦσαν	λυσάμενον	λυθέν	λελυκός	λελυμένον
	Plural	Nom.	λύοντα	λυόμενα	λύσαντα	λυσάμενα	λυθέντα	λελυκότα	λελυμένα
		Gen.	λυόντων	λυομένων	λυσάντων	λυσαμένων	λυθέντων	λελυκότων	λελυμένων
		Dat.	λύουσι(ν)	λυομένοις	λύσασι(ν)	λυσαμένοις	λυθεῖσι(ν)	λελυκόσι(ν)	λελυμένοις
		Acc.	λύοντα	λυόμενα	λύσαντα	λυσάμενα	λυθέντα	λελυκότα	λελυμένα

Subjunctive

(Aor Act. add -σ-; Aor Pass. add -θ-)

	Active		Middle/Passive	
	Sing.	Plur.	Sing.	Plur.
1st	ω	ωμεν	ωμαι	ωμεθα
2nd	ῃς	ητε	ῃ	ησθε
3rd	ῃ	ωσι(ν)	ηται	ωνται

Optative

	Active		Middle/Passive	
	Sing.	Plur.	Sing.	Plur.
1st	μι / ν	μεν	μην	μεθα
2nd	ς	τε	σο	σθε
3rd	-	εν / σαν	το	ντο

Thematic Formation:
Pres: -οι + ending
Aor A/M: -σαιη + ending
Aor P: -θειη + ending

Athematic Formation:
Pres: -ιη or -ι + ending
Aor A/M/P: -ιη or -ι + ending

Present Indicative

	Sing.	Plur.
1st	εἰμί	ἐσμέν
2nd	εἶ	ἐστέ
3rd	ἐστί(ν)	εἰσί(ν)

Imperfect Indicative

	Sing.	Plur.
1st	ἤμην	ἦμεν
2nd	ἦς	ἦτε
3rd	ἦν	ἦσαν

Future Indicative

	Sing.	Plur.
1st	ἔσομαι	ἐσόμεθα
2nd	ἔσῃ	ἔσεσθε
3rd	ἔσται	ἔσονται

Present Subjunctive

	Sing.	Plur.
1st	ὦ	ὦμεν
2nd	ᾖς	ἦτε
3rd	ᾖ	ὦσι(ν)

Present Imperative

	Sing.	Plur.
2nd	ἴσθι	ἔστε
3rd	ἔστω	ἔστωσαν

Present Optative

	Sing.	Plur.
1st	εἴην	εἶμεν/εἴημεν
2nd	εἴης	εἶτε/εἴητε
3rd	εἴη	εἶεν/εἴησαν

Infinitive

Present	εἶναι
Future	ἔσεσθαι

Present Participle

		Masc.	Fem.	Neut.
Singular	Nom.	ὤν	οὖσα	ὄν
	Gen.	ὄντος	οὔσης	ὄντος
	Dat.	ὄντι	οὔσῃ	ὄντι
	Acc.	ὄντα	οὖσαν	ὄν
Plural	Nom.	ὄντες	οὖσαι	ὄντα
	Gen.	ὄντων	οὐσῶν	ὄντων
	Dat.	οὖσι(ν)	οὔσαις	οὖσι(ν)
	Acc.	ὄντας	οὔσας	ὄντα

Definite Article

	Singular			Plural		
	Masc.	Fem.	Neut.	Masc.	Fem.	Neut.
Nom.	ὁ	ἡ	τό	οἱ	αἱ	τά
Gen.	τοῦ	τῆς	τοῦ	τῶν		
Dat.	τῷ	τῇ	τῷ	τοῖς	ταῖς	τοῖς
Acc.	τόν	τήν	τό	τούς	τάς	τά

1ˢᵗ Declension Endings

	Singular				Plur.
	ε, ι, ρ	σ, ζ, ξ, ψ	all other	Masc.	
Nom.	α	α	η	ης	αι
Gen.	ας	ης	ης	ου	ων
Dat.	ᾳ	ῃ	ῃ	ῃ	αις
Acc.	αν	αν	ην	ην	ας

2ⁿᵈ Declension Endings

	Singular			Plural		
	Masc.	Fem.	Neut.	Masc.	Fem.	Neut.
Nom.	ος		ον	οι		α
Gen.	ου			ων		
Dat.	ῳ			οις		
Acc.	ον			ους		α

3ʳᵈ Declension Endings

	Singular			Plural		
	Masc.	Fem.	Neut.	Masc.	Fem.	Neut.
Nom.	ς / -		-	ες		α
Gen.	ος			ων		
Dat.	ι			σι(ν)		
Acc.	α / ν		-	ας / ες		α

πᾶς, πᾶσα, πᾶν | 3-1-3

	Singular			Plural		
	Masc.	Fem.	Neut.	Masc.	Fem.	Neut.
Nom.	πᾶς	πᾶσα	πᾶν	πάντες	πᾶσαι	πάντα
Gen.	παντός	πάσης	παντός	πάντων	πασῶν	πάντων
Dat.	παντί	πάσῃ	παντί	πᾶσι(ν)	πάσαις	πᾶσι(ν)
Acc.	πάντα	πᾶσαν	πᾶν	πάντας	πάσας	πάντα

πολύς, πολλή, πολύ | 2-1-2

	Singular			Plural		
	Masc.	Fem.	Neut.	Masc.	Fem.	Neut.
Nom.	πολύς	πολλή	πολύ	πολλοί	πολλαί	πολλά
Gen.	πολλοῦ	πολλῆς	πολλοῦ	πολλῶν		
Dat.	πολλῷ	πολλῇ	πολλῷ	πολλοῖς	πολλαῖς	πολλοῖς
Acc.	πολύν	πολλήν	πολύ	πολλούς	πολλάς	πολλά

Personal Pronouns: *I, we, you, she, he, it, they*

| | 1st | | 2nd | | | 3rd | | | | |
| | Sing. | Plur. | Sing. | Plur. | | Singular | | | Plural | | |
						Masc.	Fem.	Neut.	Masc.	Fem.	Neut.
Nom.	ἐγώ	ἡμεῖς	σύ	ὑμεῖς	Nom.	αὐτός	αὐτή	αὐτό	αὐτοί	αὐταί	αὐτά
Gen.	(ἐ)μοῦ	ἡμῶν	σοῦ	ὑμῶν	Gen.	αὐτοῦ	αὐτῆς	αὐτοῦ	αὐτῶν		
Dat.	(ἐ)μοί	ἡμῖν	σοί	ὑμῖν	Dat.	αὐτῷ	αὐτῇ	αὐτῷ	αὐτοῖς	αὐταῖς	αὐτοῖς
Acc.	(ἐ)μέ	ἡμᾶς	σέ	ὑμᾶς	Acc.	αὐτόν	αὐτήν	αὐτό	αὐτούς	αὐτάς	αὐτά

Proximal (Near) Demonstrative: *this, these*

| | Singular | | | Plural | | |
	Masc.	Fem.	Neut.	Masc.	Fem.	Neut.
Nom.	οὗτος	αὕτη	τοῦτο	οὗτοι	αὗται	ταῦτα
Gen.	τούτου	ταύτης	τούτου	τούτων		
Dat.	τούτῳ	ταύτῃ	τούτῳ	τούτοις	ταύταις	τούτοις
Acc.	τοῦτον	ταύτην	τοῦτο	τούτους	ταύτας	ταῦτα

Distal (Far) Demonstrative: *that, those*

| | Singular | | | Plural | | |
	Masc.	Fem.	Neut.	Masc.	Fem.	Neut.
Nom.	ἐκεῖνος	ἐκείνη	ἐκεῖνο	ἐκεῖνοι	ἐκεῖναι	ἐκεῖνα
Gen.	ἐκείνου	ἐκείνης	ἐκείνου	ἐκείνων		
Dat.	ἐκείνῳ	ἐκείνῃ	ἐκείνῳ	ἐκείνοις	ἐκείναις	ἐκείνοις
Acc.	ἐκεῖνον	ἐκείνην	ἐκεῖνο	ἐκείνους	ἐκείνας	ἐκεῖνα

Interrogative Pronouns: *who? which? what?*

| | Singular | | | Plural | | |
	Masc.	Fem.	Neut.	Masc.	Fem.	Neut.
Nom.	τίς		τί	τίνες		τίνα
Gen.	τίνος			τίνων		
Dat.	τίνι			τίσι(ν)		
Acc.	τίνα		τί	τίνας		τίνα

Indefinite Pronouns: *someone, something*

| | Singular | | | Plural | | |
	Masc.	Fem.	Neut.	Masc.	Fem.	Neut.
Nom.	τις		τι	τινες		τινα
Gen.	τινος			τινων		
Dat.	τινι			τισι(ν)		
Acc.	τινα		τι	τινας		τινα

Indefinite Relative Pronouns: *whoever, whichever, every one who*

	Singular			Plural		
	Masc.	Fem.	Neut.	Masc.	Fem.	Neut.
Nom.	ὅστις	ἥτις	ὅ τι / ὅτι	οἵτινες	αἵτινες	ἅτινα
Gen.	οὗτινος	ἧστινος	οὗτινος	ὧντινων		
Dat.	ᾧτινι	ᾗτινι	ᾧτινι	οἷστισι(ν)	αἷστισι(ν)	οἷστισι(ν)
Acc.	ὅντινα	ἥντινα	ὅ τι / ὅτι	οὕστινας	ἅστινας	ἅτινα

Relative Pronouns: *who, which, that*

Reciprocal Pronouns:
one another

	Plural
Gen.	ἀλλήλων
Dat.	ἀλλήλοις
Acc.	ἀλλήλους

	Singular			Plural		
	M	F	N	M	F	N
Nom.	ὅς	ἥ	ὅ	οἵ	αἵ	ἅ
Gen.	οὗ	ἧς	οὗ	ὧν		
Dat.	ᾧ	ᾗ	ᾧ	οἷς	αἷς	οἷς
Acc.	ὅν	ἥν	ὅ	οὕς	ἅς	ἅ

Reflexive Pronouns: *myself, yourself, herself, himself, itself*

		1st		2nd		3rd		
		Masc.	Fem.	Masc.	Fem.	Masc.	Fem.	Neut.
Singular	Gen.	ἐμαυτοῦ	ἐμαυτῆς	σεαυτοῦ	σεαυτῆς	ἑαυτοῦ	ἑαυτῆς	ἑαυτοῦ
	Dat.	ἐμαυτῷ	ἐμαυτῇ	σεαυτῷ	σεαυτῇ	ἑαυτῷ	ἑαυτῇ	ἑαυτῷ
	Acc.	ἐμαυτόν	ἐμαυτήν	σεαυτόν	σεαυτήν	ἑαυτόν	ἑαυτήν	ἑαυτό
Plural	Gen.	ἑαυτῶν		ἑαυτῶν		ἑαυτῶν		
	Dat.	ἑαυτοῖς	ἑαυταῖς	ἑαυτοῖς	ἑαυταῖς	ἑαυτοῖς	ἑαυταῖς	ἑαυτοῖς
	Acc.	ἑαυτούς	ἑαυτάς	ἑαυτούς	ἑαυτάς	ἑαυτούς	ἑαυτάς	ἑαυτά